GOSPEL CLARITY

GOSPEL CLARITY

Challenging the New Perspective on Paul

William B. Barcley with Ligon Duncan

 BOOKS

EP Books
Faverdale North, Darlington, DL3 0PH, England
e-mail: sales@epbooks.org
web: www.epbooks.org

EP Books USA
P. O. Box 614, Carlisle, PA 17013, USA
e-mail: usasales@epbooks.org
web: www.epbooks.us

First published 2010

British Library Cataloguing in Publication Data available

ISBN-13 978 0 85234 733 1   ISBN 0 85234 733 2

Unless otherwise indicated, all Scripture quotations are from The Holy Bible, English Standard Version, published by HarperCollins Publishers © 2001 by Crossway Bibles, a division of Good News Publishers. Used by permission. All rights reserved.

Printed and bound in the USA

CONTENTS

PREFACE

We want to thank the many people who have encouraged or contributed to this project over the last several years. We want to thank our students at Reformed Theological Seminary who patiently listened to us lecture on the topics in this book, especially the students in our 'Paul and the Law' class in the Fall of 2003, which was where the seeds of this book were planted. Our friend and colleague Dr John Currid first encouraged us to turn the lectures from that class into a book, and as a board member at Evangelical Press recommended the project. David Clark, formerly of EP, was a firm believer in the importance of this book and especially of the need for gospel clarity in the churches in England, where the New Perspective on Paul has caused much confusion. He was a tremendous encouragement in the early stages of this work. David Woollin has picked up the mantle and has continued to guide and to spur us towards publication. Thanks, too, to Anne Williamson for her careful and thorough editing. It is a joy to work with an editor who has a grasp both of the theological issues presented in this book and of how best to express them in a clear and compelling way.

Nick Reed, who served at different times as student assistant to both of us, did a wonderful job of pulling resources together for the chapters on justification. His work helped lay the foundation for that section of the book.

Several colleagues and friends read parts or all of this manuscript and gave invaluable feedback: Dr Charles Wingard, Senior Pastor of Westminster Presbyterian Church in Huntsville, Alabama; Dr John Currid, Derek Thomas, Guy

Waters and Bob Cara, all of Reformed Theological Seminary; and Dr Carl Trueman of Westminster Theological Seminary. We are grateful for their encouragement, as well as for their helpful critique.

We believe the issues at the heart of the debate over the New Perspective on Paul have eternal consequences. May God use this debate and this book to bring people to a greater understanding of his truth, as well as of the one who is the way, the truth, and the life.

INTRODUCTION

Has the evangelical church misread Paul? Did the Reformers
get it wrong when they used Paul in battling against the
perceived errors of Roman Catholicism? Was the Reformation itself, then, in error, not only mishandling the Bible,
but also causing great damage to the cause of Christ by
bringing division to the church, whereas Paul strove for unity?
These are the key questions that have been raised by the so-
called 'New Perspective on Paul'.

The phrase 'New Perspective on Paul' (hereafter referred
to as 'NPP') is one that was coined by one of its proponents
and is a way of looking at first-century Judaism and Paul's
writings that differs significantly from traditional Reformed
and evangelical interpretations. Many of the proponents of
the NPP are explicit in their desire to free the writings of the
Bible, and Paul's letters in particular, from their 'Lutheran
captivity'. According to the NPP, two key factors have driven
the evangelical interpretation of Paul since the Reformation.
They are, firstly, Luther's angst and struggle with the question,
'How can a sinner be right with a holy God?'; and, secondly,
his battle with the perceived legalism and works-righteousness
of medieval Roman Catholicism. According to the NPP,
Luther and the evangelical church ever since have read Paul
wrongly through these particular lenses.

The monk Luther struggled with his sin. This led him to
wrestle mightily with Paul's phrase 'the righteousness of God'
(Rom. 1:17). Luther hated that phrase because he believed it

was a standard that he could not attain. He hated it, that is, until he came to the conclusion that Paul's phrase 'the right-eousness of God' referred to the free gift of righteousness that God gives to sinners who trust Jesus Christ alone for salvation.

According to the NPP, however, Paul's struggle was not Luther's struggle. Paul was not driven by the question of how a sinner can be in a right relationship with God. Rather, the driving force in Paul's life was his call to be the apostle to the Gentiles, and the key question was how Gentiles can be 'grafted in' to what is at its root the Jewish religion. The primary issue for Paul, then, was not one's standing with God (though many proponents of the NPP do not deny its impor-tance). Rather, he was wrestling with questions of community (the church) and the creation of one body — composed of Jews and Gentiles — living together in unity. Proponents of the NPP differ in their formulations of how they get here. But the NPP holds in common the assertion that the bringing together of Jews and Gentiles into the single family of God was central to Paul's letters.

The second key factor in Luther's reading of Paul was his opposition to Roman Catholic teaching on penance, indul-gences and the meritorious place of works in justification. According to Luther, Roman Catholic teaching had distorted the gospel message and taught a false gospel of works-righteousness legalism — that is, our works contribute to a right standing with God. Here again, the NPP argues, Luther read Paul in the light of his own situation. When Paul pits 'justification by faith' over against 'works of the law', Luther believed that Paul was battling against Jewish (or Jewish Christian) legalism. But, the NPP claims, this is both to misun-derstand Paul and to misunderstand first-century Judaism.

According to the NPP, first-century Judaism was not a religion of legalistic 'works-righteousness' in which Jews believed they earned favour with God by their good deeds. Instead, first-century Judaism was a religion of grace. As a result, when Paul places 'justification by faith' over against 'works of the law', he is not battling against legalism. Rather, he is in contention with those who want to uphold Jewish boundary markers that set Jews apart from Gentiles. Here again, then, we see the communal emphasis. 'Works of the law' divide Jews and Gentiles. That is Paul's central problem with these 'works' — not that they impose a rival view of how a sinner can be right with a holy God.

A further key point in the NPP is that Paul's religion as a Christian is not as radically distinct from his Jewish background as has commonly been thought. Paul must be read, the NPP asserts, in the light of, not over against, the Judaism of his day. This includes key terms (such as 'righteousness') and his overall outlook. One writer sums up the NPP by saying that it 'narrows the distance between Paul and the Judaism of his day while it widens the gap between Paul and the Reformation'.[1]

The result is that the NPP has radically redefined several words and theological concepts that evangelical Christians have long thought they understood. These include 'gospel', 'justification', 'faith', 'works of the law', and even the nature of 'grace'. In fact, we can say that the 'new perspective' does not just affect one's reading of Paul, but it redefines biblical religion. Justification, and the status of an individual sinner with a holy God, has been moved out of the centre of both Pauline and biblical teaching. Grace, while remaining central to the NPP, has lost much of the nuance and specificity that it has garnered in the Reformed tradition.

For instance, one of the examples that the NPP gives to show that Judaism was a religion of grace is that God gave sacrifices to deal with sin. But, according to the New Testament, the blood of bulls and goats cannot take away sin. Sacrifices cleanse the flesh, but ultimately serve as a reminder of ever-present sin, while pointing to the only sufficient sacrifice for sin in the death of Jesus Christ. While we agree with, and appreciate, the NPP's emphasis that God's covenants with Israel, including the Mosaic covenant, were gracious, the failure to show precisely what this grace looks like and the place it plays in the life of faith leads, in our view, to serious errors. 'Grace', in their writings, often looks very much like a synergistic ('working together') movement, in which God helps sinful human beings to cooperate in salvation, rather than a monergistic (God working alone) rescue operation in which God pulls helpless sinners out of the fire of hell.

To be fair, there are significant differences between the leading proponents of the NPP. Some are not confessing Christians. Others belong to the liberal wing of Christianity that denies doctrines like the deity of Christ, the inspiration of Scripture, penal, substitutionary atonement and the necessity of faith in Christ for salvation. Still others are a lot closer to evangelical and Reformed Christianity. N. T. Wright, for instance, has more in common with evangelicalism than, say, E. P. Sanders, even placing himself within the Reformed tradition. Wright's formulations are often helpful, even inspiring. He upholds many vital evangelical doctrines relating to salvation in Christ.

But even in Wright, with the rest of the NPP, the weight in reading Paul falls strongly on communal concerns. According to Wright, for instance, justification is not about how one establishes a relationship with God. Nor is it about how one becomes a member of the covenant people. Rather, it is about 'how you could tell who was in. In standard Christian theological language, it wasn't so much about soteriology as about ecclesiology; not so much about salvation as about the church.'[2] Wright calls justification 'the great ecumenical doctrine'. Similarly, for Wright the gospel is not the good news that sinners can be right with God by trusting in Jesus Christ and his finished work. As he puts it, 'the gospel' is not 'a message about "how one gets saved", in an individual and ahistorical sense'.[3] It is, at its heart, the proclamation that Jesus is Lord.

Thus, while differences do exist among the leading proponents of the NPP, there is a strong core of agreement. While it is certainly correct, as some have done, to refer to the 'new *perspectives* on Paul', and to do the important work of analysing each of the leading proponents separately,[4] that is not the task of this book. Our goal is to examine the NPP as a movement among modern scholars, and to clarify the nature of that movement. The focus is more on the development of key themes within the NPP, rather than discussing the nuances of the various scholars involved. Instead of chapters devoted to individuals, the chapters of this book focus on themes. To be sure, we interact with key scholars along the way, but detailed interaction with the leading proponents of the NPP is not the goal.

The NPP has brought much confusion to the church of Jesus Christ. As pastors who are also scholars (one a trained New Testament scholar, the other a trained theologian), we grieve over that result. Confused Christians lack assurance, prove to be unfruitful and are in a place of spiritual danger. Likewise, the gospel of Jesus Christ is the power of God unto salvation, but when that gospel is watered down or distorted it becomes ineffective. It loses its power to save. Thus, when anyone comes along proclaiming a different gospel (including a different definition of what 'the gospel' is), it must be carefully examined.

This book began as a class we taught together at Reformed Theological Seminary, Jackson, Mississippi, in the Fall of 2003, called 'Paul and the Law'. That course focused on the use of 'law' in Paul's letters, examined 'law' in the light of broader biblical covenant theology, and along the way interacted with the NPP. Evangelical Press heard about the course and asked us to take our material and turn it into a book, especially focusing on the NPP.

The publisher asked us to write this book *from* a traditional Reformed perspective (which was relatively easy) and *for* a broad audience (which was extremely difficult). This book seeks to lay out the basic teaching of the NPP in a way that is accessible to ordinary, educated Christians. The goal is not a

detailed critique of the NPP or of its individual proponents
(though critique is certainly present — even abundant —
along the way). Rather, the goal is to affirm for God's people
the truth of basic Reformed theology and to show how the
NPP is a dangerous departure both from good exegesis and
from orthodox biblical teaching. Ultimately what we desire is
that God's people should have clarity on matters of essential
Christian doctrine.

This book has been several years in the making, in large
part because of busy lives, a move and the beginning of a new
ministry, and various other commitments. Much of the work
on which it is based was carried out in preparation for the
class taught several years ago. In the intervening years, however, several significant publications by and about the proponents of the NPP have emerged. Most significant has been
the interaction between John Piper and N. T. Wright on
justification.[5] We have benefited from this interaction, and
especially from Wright's attempt to clarify his position —
though, at the end of the day, little has changed from what he
has really said all along.

Because of the high-profile nature of this debate, the
importance of the doctrine of justification and the significant
inroads that Wright has made into the evangelical community,
we have devoted two chapters (chapters 5 and 6) to justification. These chapters, which interact with Wright's views, are
the most detailed and complex sections of the book. Wright in
particular claims that he has been misread, especially that his
critics have failed to read his formulations in the light of the
larger biblical 'story' that he believes would have been foundational for Paul. It is, he asserts, 'just as if I'd never said it'. We
have taken that seriously and attempted to approach him
precisely where he wants his readers to begin. To be sure,
Wright's narrative and covenantal approach set him apart from
the other leading proponents of the NPP. But at the end of the
day we believe his formulations are a misreading of the covenantal structure of the Bible, of justification and of the central

biblical message. We beg the reader's patience as we attempt to set out our critique in those chapters. They do not contain only critique, however, as along the way we also present the traditional Reformed doctrine of justification by grace alone through faith alone in Christ alone to the glory of God alone.

We pray that in the pages of this book God's people may again hear the gospel message, the good news that Christ Jesus came into the world to save sinners. We are convinced that the most important question that a person can ask is, 'How can a sinner be in a right relationship with a holy and just God?' Indeed, we are convinced that this is the central theme of the Bible. This is not to downplay the corporate and cosmic nature of God's redemptive work. When God calls his elect ones to himself, he always puts them in community. The return of Jesus Christ with power and glory will mean the liberation of this world and the coming of a new heaven and a new earth. But these communal and cosmic aspects cannot take precedence over the question of how an individual sinner, whose life has been an affront to a holy God, can be reconciled to God and become a part of the redeemed and renewed people of God. Christ builds his church as individuals repent, turning from their sin, and trust in Jesus Christ alone for salvation. The coming of the new creation begins with the transformation of the human heart: 'If anyone is in Christ, he is a new creation. The old has passed away; behold, the new has come' (2 Cor. 5:17). The question of the Philippian jailer, 'What must I do to be saved?' is still the central question that the biblical record compels individuals to ask.

Our prayer is that the teaching of God's Word and the truth of salvation and justification in Christ come alive in new and exciting ways and that, instead of confusion, God's people may have clarity, confidence, hope and assurance. The apostle Paul said it best: 'Since we have been justified by faith … we rejoice in hope of the glory of God' (Rom. 5:1-2).

1.

AN OVERVIEW OF THE NEW PERSPECTIVE ON PAUL

In many ways, the 'new perspective' is not all that new. While NPP writings contain several novel interpretations of Pauline words and phrases, most of the ideas that make up the foundation of the new perspective were actually put forward by interpreters of the Bible many years earlier. But they have recently taken hold — seemingly, for two reasons. The first is the thorough, thoughtful and persuasive way in which they have been presented. The leading proponents of the NPP are outstanding scholars and good communicators — learned, creative, clear, winsome and witty. The second reason for the popularity of the NPP is that it coincides with impulses current in society that are compatible with it — indeed, that are even demanded in some circles. These impulses include the contemporary social virtues of tolerance, unity and ecumenism. In a post-Holocaust world, there is an understandable desire to remove from the church all semblance of anti-Semitism. The NPP fits in well with the modern attempt to bring together Judaism and Christianity, Protestantism and Catholicism.

This is not to say that the NPP has simply read the Bible in the light of modern sensibilities and so should be dismissed out of hand. It is possible that the modern world has made us sensitive to certain realities and enabled us to see what was there all along, but that we were missing. Thus we need to take a careful look at the key ideas of the NPP and how they have developed in recent scholarship. This chapter is devoted to that task.

As we examine the development of thought within the NPP, we see that there is a logic to it that cannot easily be dismissed. Indeed, there is much that is good and helpful in the NPP. Readers need to appreciate and feel the weight of this before we enter into detailed disagreement. Thus this chapter attempts to lay out the development of the central ideas of the NPP, with only minor critique. We will save the bulk of our assessment for the chapters that follow.

IDEAS CENTRAL TO THE NPP

Some of the key ideas in the development of the NPP are as follows:

1. Paul had a robust conscience

One of the assertions that set off an 'anti-Lutheran' rereading of Paul's letters was that Paul was not plagued by a guilty, introspective conscience, but rather demonstrated a robust conscience. Ironically, this assertion was made by a Lutheran minister and one-time Lutheran Bishop of Stockholm, Krister Stendahl.[1] Stendahl took his cues from passages like Philippians 3:6, where Paul claims that he was 'blameless' with regard to the righteousness in the law.

Stendahl contrasts this with the experience of Luther, who struggled with his own sinfulness and wrestled with the question, 'How can a sinner be justified in the sight of a holy God?' In other words, Stendahl argued, Paul's central concern was not, 'How can sinners be saved?' Rather, Paul's central concern was driven by his 'call'.

2. Paul was 'called' to be the apostle to the Gentiles, and this became his primary concern

Stendahl is insistent that we understand the dramatic change in Paul's life as a 'call' to the Gentile mission, not a 'conversion' to a new religion.[2] Paul was a Jew, and never gave up his essential identity as a Jew. He did believe, contrary to most Jews of his day, that the Messiah had come, and this belief led to theological diversions from first-century Judaism. But, on the whole, Paul did not change religions. He changed the course of his life.

Now Paul's life was driven by his call to be the 'apostle to the Gentiles'. The driving question for him, then, became, 'How can Gentiles be included in the people of God? How can Jews and "unclean" Gentile "sinners" be one in the body of Christ?' It is this concern that drove Paul's development of his theology, not the problem of how sinners can be saved. Of course, this potentially has major implications for understanding some of Paul's key theological terms, such as 'justification', which Stendahl does not believe to be a central Pauline doctrine. Rather, the concept of 'justification by faith, not works of the law' was developed by Paul to deal with the issue of the inclusion of the Gentiles and their unity with Jewish believers. We will return to this later. But Stendahl's insights laid the groundwork for a 'paradigm shift' (to use the language of Thomas Kuhn) in Pauline studies, though Stendahl himself did not systematically work out all the implications of his findings. That was left for others.

3. First-century Judaism was not a religion of legalistic self-righteousness

In 1977 the bombshell was dropped with the publication of E. P. Sanders' work, *Paul and Palestinian Judaism*.[3] Sanders' book is a monumental study of the writings of first-century Jews, in particular 'Palestinian' Jews, or Jews who lived in the land of Israel. His exhaustive study leads Sanders to conclude that first-century Jews did not believe they were saved by their own works, in the sense of building up merit with God. Rather, the 'pattern of religion' (as Sanders calls it) of first-century Judaism was that of 'covenantal nomism'. Jews were saved, Sanders argued, because they were part of the covenant people. They kept the law ('nomism', from the Greek word *nomos*, meaning 'law') for two reasons. Firstly, it was a response to God's gracious act in choosing them to be his people. Secondly, the keeping of the law maintained their status in the covenant. So, as Sanders put it, obedience to the law does not get you in, but it does keep you in. Those who lack covenant faithfulness will be cut off from the people of God.

Sanders argued that first-century Judaism was a religion of grace in which God chose Israel, enabled obedience and made provision for disobedience in sacrifices. Jews by and large did not hold to a 'works-righteousness' legalism, by which their good deeds earned their standing before God.

Paul's pattern of religion, by contrast, while having affinities with Judaism with regard to getting in and staying in, was that of 'participationist eschatology'. In other words, according to Sanders, the coming of Messiah means that the end times have broken into the present. Believers partake of eschatological life by participating with, or being united to, Christ. Thus the notion of the believer's union with Christ is prominent in Paul's letters ('in Christ', 'Christ in you', dying and rising 'with Christ', etc.). For Paul, according to Sanders, the biggest danger for believers is the avoidance of unions that break, or are inconsistent with, the believer's union with Christ.

Sanders' reading of first-century Judaism in particular is the starting point of what many have termed the 'Sanders revolution'. It is the foundation for the new perspective. Scholars like N. T. Wright, for example, assert that Sanders' conclusions about first-century Judaism are 'established'.[4] His findings, then, form the presuppositional base that informs their reading of Paul, even though many have significant disagreements with Sanders over how to read Paul in the light of his conclusions. We shall see some of the outworking of this in the following section.

4. Therefore, Paul was not refuting Jewish legalism

If first-century Judaism was not legalistic (in Sanders' sense of building up merit to attain favour with God), then Paul could not have been refuting Jewish legalism, as has been tradition-ally taught. Paul did not place justification by faith over against 'law', or 'works of the law', because Jews saw law obedience as a means to salvation. Rather, according to Sanders, since life under the law was characteristic of Judaism, Paul is simply arguing that one does not have to be a Jew to be righteous. In short, Sanders asserts, Paul's problem with Judaism was that it was not Christianity.

It is at this point that James Dunn enters the fray. Dunn was persuaded by Sanders' work, but found this last point to be deficient. In other words, it was not enough, according to Dunn, to say simply that Paul's argument with Judaism was that it was not Christianity. At the same time, Sanders' work had convinced Dunn that Paul's opposition to 'works of the law' was not a refutation of legalism.

Dunn proposed a different interpretation of Paul's phrase 'works of the law'. He claimed that it does not refer to Jewish efforts to keep the law and thereby earn their salvation. Rather, the term 'works of the law' refers to those aspects of the law that are distinctly Jewish and that separate Jews from Gentiles.[5] Dunn acknowledged that 'works of the law' can refer to all that the law requires. But when the context is that of Jewish relations with the nations, the phrase focuses more specifically on those laws that serve as 'boundary markers' for Jews. In particular, the 'works of the law' are circumcision, food laws and Sabbath observance. Paul's problem with 'works of the law', then, according to Dunn, is that they are banners of Jewish nationalism and are waved specifically to exclude Gentiles. Paul opposes Judaism for its exclusivity — Jew against Gentile — not for its legalistic, works-righteousness mentality. Instead of actively pursuing their own individualistic righteousness, Jews were resting in their coven-antal status and boasting in their election as God's people. Nationalism, not legalism, was the problem.

This interpretation, of course, fits well with what we have seen earlier about Paul's call to the Gentile mission. Paul's work as 'apostle to the Gentiles' would be severely undercut if Gentiles were excluded from full fellowship with Jews in the church and were seen as in some way second-class Christians. Thus Paul battled to break down the barriers between Jewish Christians and Gentile Christians. Jewish Christians who insisted that Gentiles be circumcised and obey food laws were essentially saying that Gentiles needed to become Jews. This would undercut the integrity of Gentiles and the unity of the body of Christ.

We will come back to Dunn's interpretation of the phrase 'works of the law', but we can say that there is much good in his interpretation at this point. Paul does indeed desire full unity between Jewish and Gentile believers in the body of Christ. Numerous places in Paul's letters bear this out (cf., e.g., Eph. 2:11-22). But we will need to explore whether this social dimension, Jew and Gentile together in the body of Christ, is indeed Paul's central concern. For instance, when Paul attacks his Galatian opponents' insistence on circum-cision, is he primarily consumed with social concerns, as Dunn and other proponents of the NPP assert? Or does Paul see salvation itself as being at stake in a gospel that teaches justification by faith plus works, as the Reformers understood it?

5. In the light of this, Paul's problem with the law was not that it could not save, or that the Jews had misunderstood it with respect to salvation

Traditional Reformed theology has taught a threefold use of the Mosaic law in Scripture. First, the law was given to reveal God's standards of righteousness, and so to serve as a moral guide, particularly to the old-covenant people, and to restrain evil. Secondly, the law was intended to show us our sin, to convict, and to lead us to Christ. Thirdly, the law was meant to be a guide to believers to instruct them in holiness. Lutherans and dispensationalists, who pose a strong law-gospel antithesis, have traditionally agreed with the first two of these uses, but not with the third one. Proponents of the NPP typically do not disagree with the first and third uses of the law. They do, however, take issue with the second one.

Sanders argued, coining a phrase that has now become standard among many proponents of the NPP,[6] that Paul reasoned 'from solution to plight'. In other words, Paul's thinking did not go from the plight of sin to the solution of a Saviour, Jesus Christ. Rather, Paul came to believe that Jesus was the long-awaited Messiah, and so reasoned backward to the plight of man, particularly of the Jew under the law. What is that plight? Again, for Sanders it is that Jews who remain under law fail to embrace Christ. For Dunn, it is an inappropriate 'zeal', an allegiance to the law that excludes Gentiles (like that of Saul of Tarsus).

For key proponents of the NPP, then, Paul's major problem with the law is not its inability to save, nor is it in Jewish misunderstanding of the law as a means to salvation. The new perspective teaches that Paul does not say the problem with the law is inability to keep the law. Indeed, the law itself is filled with grace — God graciously entered into a covenant relationship with the Jews and graciously provided sacrifices as a means of atoning for their sin. Judaism, the NPP says, is as much a religion of grace as Christianity. At the same time, the Jews in Paul's day understood the law to teach grace, not salvation by accumulating merit. They may have misunderstood the law as teaching exclusivity (as Dunn claims), but they did not come to believe that the law actually promoted works-righteousness.

Sanders does at this point recognize some strands of first-century Palestinian Judaism as having a 'works-righteousness' mindset. Yet he treats this as a minority opinion, not that of mainstream Judaism.

Here again there is much to appreciate in the NPP. Historically, Paul did indeed move from solution to plight, from the Damascus Road revelation of Christ to deeper reflection on the plight of man. But does this reflection not lead him to understand the profound insight that all are under sin's tyranny, and that humanity's great problem is the guilt and power of sin? Furthermore, the NPP's emphasis on the grace of the law is helpful. In fact, traditional Reformed theology has always taught that the Mosaic covenant was gracious, as an extension of the covenant of grace made with Abraham. The NPP rejects a strong law-gospel contrast, emphasizing the goodness of the law and, for some of its proponents, even recognizing the value of the law in Paul's ethical injunctions. Having said that, we need to look with care at Paul's statements concerning the law to determine whether inability to keep the law plays a part and whether there is evidence that he saw the Jews as misunderstanding the law's teaching with regard to salvation.

IMPLICATIONS FOR JUSTIFICATION BY FAITH

All of the above have direct ramifications for the traditional Protestant and Reformed doctrine of justification by faith alone.

First, this new direction has *shifted justification by faith away from the centre of Paul's theology and gospel.* As Wright puts it, justification by faith 'was not the main thrust of his evangelistic message',[7] referring to it elsewhere as a 'second-order doctrine'.[8] Some have even gone so far as to call justification a 'subsidiary crater'[9] in Paul's thought, developed only to address the issue of how Jews and Gentiles can coexist in the body of Christ. This is a logical extension of the belief that Paul's main concern was not, 'How can a sinner be saved before a holy God?', but rather, 'How can Gentiles be included in the church?'

Secondly, the redefinition of first-century Judaism, and in particular of the phrase 'works of the law', logically leads to *a new understanding of justification by faith*. In Romans and Galatians, Paul contrasts justification by faith with 'works of the law'. Traditionally, this phrase in Paul's writings has been seen as the Jewish attempt to be saved by law-keeping, over against which the apostle argues for the necessity of faith alone. But if Jews did not believe their works saved them, and if 'works of the law' refers primarily to badges of Jewish nationalism, naturally it is foolish to think that Paul was opposing something that did not exist.

When it comes to defining justification, the proponents of the NPP differ with one another. Sanders, for example, while attempting to shift justification from the centre of Paul's thought, argues that Paul somewhat inconsistently puts forward both a 'forensic' strand of thought (law-court language) and a 'participationist' one (see the earlier discussion of Sanders' view of Paul's theology). According to Sanders, Paul uses justification primarily as 'transfer terminology', and sees a transformative aspect to it.

A more thorough description of justification comes from N. T. Wright. He argues that Paul's terminology relating to justification must be seen in the light of the Judaism of his day. The Jews looked forward to a day when God would defeat their enemies, bring a new exodus from their current state of exile (they were in the land, but not yet free from foreign domination) and vindicate them, proving them to be the true worshippers of the one true living God. In the first-century context, then, justification is eschatological (the fulfilment of God's end-time promises), forensic (God's legal declaration that they are 'in the right') and covenantal (demonstrating God's faithfulness to his covenant with Israel).[10] Justification is the language of the law-court, when God declares his people to be innocent. This happens at the end of history and is based on God's covenant with his people Israel. The vindicated ones are those who prove themselves to be faithful to the covenant, refusing to bow down and worship idols, but remaining loyal to Yahweh.

According to Wright, the phrase 'the righteousness of God' (e.g., Rom. 1:17) refers to God's covenant faithfulness, not his own moral righteousness or the status that he bestows on sinners. Similarly, in his view, justification, especially as it appears in Paul's letters, is not primarily about soteriology, but ecclesiology — that is, we should see it not primarily in terms of salvation, but in terms of the church. Justification is not a doctrine about how one gets saved, but rather how you know someone is part of the people of God. Or, to put it differently, 'justification is not how someone *becomes* a Christian. It is a declaration that they *have become* a Christian.'[11] In justification, God vindicates his people by declaring that they are 'in the right', belonging to him as proven by their faithfulness.

Wright provocatively argues that justification, as the great ecclesiastical and ecumenical doctrine, has been taken over by the church and twisted into its opposite. He claims that Romans and Galatians, the two principal letters in which Paul expounds the doctrine of justification by faith, deal primarily with the question of who is part of the people of God. The key issue is table fellowship — 'With whom can I, must I, share table fellowship?' Paul's answer is that in justification God declares both faithful Jews and faithful Gentiles to be part of the body of Christ, and so both partake of Christ and share table fellowship together. The church since Paul's day, however, has taken justification and made it a doctrine that divides Christians, particularly Protestants and Roman Catholics. All who believe in Jesus, Wright asserts, are declared in justification to be in the right and so should be united with one another.[12]

A few final points regarding justification. The proponents of the NPP *deny the doctrine of the imputation of Christ's righteousness*, a doctrine that has been increasingly under attack within evangelical circles. Wright argues that in Jewish legal terminology the righteousness of a judge, or of anyone else for that matter, cannot be transferred across a courtroom and imputed to someone else. As Wright puts it, 'that is not how the language works'.[13] Justification is a simple legal declaration that someone is 'in the right'.

In addition, proponents of the NPP have largely *redefined faith* away from its traditional Reformational meaning. Traditionally, Reformed and evangelical Christians have understood saving faith to include three elements — knowledge, assent and trust. For true saving faith to be present a believer must know certain things about God, Jesus Christ and God's provision of salvation in Christ. He must be convicted of the truth of these matters and give his assent to them. And he must trust Christ alone to save him. Faith, furthermore, has been understood to be 'the alone instrument of justification'.[14] In the NPP, faith is redefined and described in various ways. It has come to be seen simply as an identity marker or badge of covenant membership, set over against circumcision, that marks off who belongs to the church. In the NPP, we also see faith defined as 'faithfulness'. In this sense, faith appears to be more than trusting in God to save you and to incorporate perseverance and obedience to the commands of God, which of course fits with Sanders' understanding of Jewish 'covenantal nomism'.

CONCLUSION

It is clear from all of the above that the New Perspective on Paul presents a tremendous challenge to the traditional reading of Paul's letters and to the key doctrines of the Reformation. The new perspective, in the light of its reading of first-century Judaism and Paul's call to be the apostle to the Gentiles, has taken doctrines that the church has typically understood to relate to individuals with regard to the problem of sin (though with clear implications for the body of Christ and for mission) and has redefined them in ways that are largely corporate and social. In this sense, the NPP has a coherence and a consistency that give it plausibility. It is also important to point out that many of the proponents of the NPP do not deny the problem of sin, nor do they deny the need for individual forgiveness of sins. They simply assert that the church has misunderstood many key terms, like 'justification'. The reason for this, they argue, is that earlier Christians were not reading Paul in the light of what we now know of first-century Judaism. Rather, they were reading him in terms of their own historical circumstances, such as medieval Catholicism and its practice of indulgences. What is needed, they say, is to look at Paul's letters afresh and, in the light of recent historical advances, particularly with regard to our understanding of first-century Judaism.[15]

We will challenge the NPP on many fronts. Historically, we will ask whether first-century Judaism was indeed as free from legalism as the NPP proponents claim. Exegetically (that is, having to do with the interpretation of biblical texts), we will look closely at biblical teaching to see if their conclusions are warranted by the text. Theologically, we will look at the implications and problems of the views of these scholars for Christian belief. But we will begin by looking at a crucial question: what was the effect of Paul's conversion and call to preach to the Gentiles on his life and teaching? We turn to that now.

2.

THE ORIGIN OF PAUL'S CHRISTIAN LIFE AND GOSPEL

Three issues are at the heart of the NPP's reinterpretation of Paul's letters. They are, first, the nature of first-century Judaism and Paul's relation to it; secondly, the effect of Paul's call to be the 'apostle to the Gentiles' on his life and ministry; and, thirdly, the nature of Paul's gospel in view of the above. We will look more closely at the NPP's reading of first-century Judaism in the following chapter. The more fundamental issues revolve around Paul's call and his gospel.

One of the fundamental presuppositions of the NPP is that, on the road to Damascus, Paul was not 'converted'; he was 'called' to be the apostle to the Gentiles. Krister Stendahl put this most forcefully in his writings between thirty and forty years ago, but this interpretation has been echoed in various ways by NPP proponents ever since. We see it, for instance, in statements to the effect that Paul did not leave Judaism for something else. He remained a Jew, albeit one who believed that the Messiah had come. Paul was therefore not converted to a new religion; he was called to be a 'light to the nations', to take the gospel to the Gentiles. That gospel, furthermore, proclaimed that 'the crucified and risen Jesus is Lord' (as Wright puts it). Its focus is not on how individual sinners can be right with God (justified, in the traditional sense). Rather, it declares that through the Jewish Messiah God is establishing his rule over the whole world and describes how Jews and

Gentiles can be one in the congregation of those who believe in Jesus, the Jewish Messiah.[1]

If there has been a radical shift in Paul's life, it is that he has gone from being Saul, the violent exclusivist, to Paul, the non-violent universalist. In other words, Saul the Pharisee once rigorously observed the Torah and sought to keep Judaism pure from all Gentile influence. This led him to persecute those Jews who failed to observe Torah with the same rigour, as well as to persecute any who threatened the purity of Judaism. Now Paul the apostle has come to recognize that God's plan to reach the Gentiles is being fulfilled, and that Gentiles are to be included in the people of God apart from specific Jewish boundary markers.

This reconstruction of Paul's life and ministry may be helpful in bringing out aspects of Paul's letters that have often been overlooked by interpreters of the Bible. But it truncates Paul's letters and shifts the focus of his thought from what is primary to what is secondary (which is not to say unimportant). As such, it is a distortion of Paul's teaching and his gospel. We will proceed by looking first at Paul's conversion and its impact on his life and ministry. Then we will examine specifically the impact of this on his gospel, asking the question: what is the nature of the gospel that Paul proclaimed?

THE ROAD FROM DAMASCUS

What effect did Paul's experience on the road to Damascus have on his life and ministry? Is it proper to speak of that experience as a 'conversion', a 'call', or some combination of the two?

The traditional view of Paul's experience on the road to Damascus is that he had a transforming encounter with the living Christ in which Paul came to know the grace of God reaching out to the 'chief of sinners'. In that experience Paul was drawn into a living relationship with Jesus as the crucified, resurrected and ascended Messiah. He saw his own sinfulness in his persecution of Christ's body, the church, which in turn enabled him to reflect more deeply on his sin and need for a Saviour. He recognized the futility of his own efforts to achieve his salvation. And he received his commission to preach Christ to the Gentiles, which included a call to suffer for Christ's sake. Paul also received the gospel that he was to preach both to Jews and to Gentiles (Gal. 1:11-12).

The NPP shifts the emphasis away from God's grace shown to Paul the sinner to Paul's recognition of God's plan to include the Gentiles and of his call to be a light to the Gentiles. James Dunn, one of the leading proponents of the NPP, puts it this way:

> ... what Paul experienced [on the road to Damascus] was not so much his acceptance as one who had previously been without acceptance by God, but primarily the shattering of his assumption that righteousness before God was Israel's peculiar privilege and his corollary assumption that those who threatened Israel's set-apartness to God, by preaching Messiah Jesus to Gentiles, had to be persecuted.[2]

Here we see two essential assumptions of the new perspective. The first is that primary for Paul was his recognition that God's redemptive work included the Gentiles and was not confined to national, ethnic Israel. This leads in turn to the assertion of Dunn, Wright *et al.* that Paul's critique of the Jews in his letters was not with respect to their legalism, but related to their nationalism — Jews over against Gentiles. The second assumption is that Paul's primary sin was his violent 'zeal' that led to the persecution of Jews and Hellenistic Christians who were a threat to Israel's boundaries and distinctiveness. Though Dunn seems to prefer the language of 'call' over 'conversion',[3] he uses the term 'conversion' to describe Paul's dramatic shift away from his former 'zeal'.[4]

Dunn asserts that on the road to Damascus Paul did not, as it were, experience God's grace for the first time. Judaism in Paul's day was a religion of grace, the new perspective proponents assert, and so Paul had known and lived by God's grace. But Paul came to realize that he had obscured and perverted that grace. His experience on the Damascus Road taught him 'the more basic insight of God's grace: as free grace it was open to all and not restricted to Jews and their proselytes'.[5]

These assertions, though containing some elements of truth, miss the central thrust of Paul's letters and of his own testimony to his conversion. To begin with, it is true that when Paul talks about his Damascus Road experience in, for example, Galatians 1:15-17, he does so with respect to God's 'call'. Paul was indeed called to be the apostle to the Gentiles. But it is not an either/or; it is both/and. Paul was both called and converted. In fact, in Paul's letters, God's 'call' is always closely associated with conversion.

Paul consistently describes his converts as having been 'called' (1 Cor. 1:9,26; Gal. 1:6; Eph. 4:4; etc.). Romans 9:24 is especially instructive because it refers to both Jewish and Gentile converts to Christianity as having been called. If both Jews and Gentiles are similarly called, this blunts the force of the argument of NPP advocates who say that Paul did not see Jewish Christians as having been converted to a different religion. For Paul, both Jews and Gentiles needed to be called out of unbelief and into the hope of the gospel. This 'effective call' to believe in Christ also included a call to serve Christ. Paul had a unique 'call' to be the apostle to the Gentiles. Yet all believers are called in the sense of being transformed by Christ and set apart to follow and serve Christ.

In fact, Paul experienced a radical conversion and transformation in his life and in his theological understanding. Even a partial list of evidence from his letters will show the far-reaching impact of the Damascus Road experience.

1. Paul experienced a transforming encounter with the living Christ

In Galatians 1:16, Paul talks about his Damascus Road experience as Christ being revealed 'in me' (NASB, NIV, KJV). Some translations read 'to me'. This is possible, but unlikely given the fact that Paul uses similar language only a chapter later, in Galatians 2:20, where he states, 'I have been crucified with Christ. It is no longer I who live, but Christ who lives in me. And the life I now live in the flesh I live by faith in the Son of God, who loved me and gave himself for me.' The revelation of Christ in him surely refers in part to Paul's evangelistic work in making Christ known. But at a basic and profound level it means that Paul has entered into a faith union with the living Christ that has transformed his previous existence. Christ has inwardly, by his Spirit (cf. Rom. 8:9-11), taken up residence in Paul and brought about a new creation (2 Cor. 5:17; Gal. 6:15).

2. Paul's experience with the living Christ transformed his eschatology and, therefore, his theology

Paul's encounter with Christ led him to the recognition that the Messiah had indeed come. But instead of coming in victory over Israel's physical enemies, as the Jews had anticipated, Christ was rejected and put to death on a cross. Yet, unbeknown to Christ's enemies, this death was itself a victory — first, because it appeased God's wrath and brought reconciliation between God and his elect; and, secondly, because in his death he triumphed over sin and over God's spiritual enemies. Furthermore, he rose again, triumphing over death, and then ascended to the right hand of God, where he reigns until all his enemies are subdued under him. The social and political hopes which dominated Paul's thinking as a Jew become largely spiritual, but with profound social and political implications.

At the same time, the recognition that the ascended Lord
is the Messiah means that the long-awaited end times have
arrived. The last days are here, but not yet in their fulness.
Jesus himself had proclaimed that the kingdom of God had
arrived in his life and ministry (e.g., Luke 11:20; Mark 1:15),
and yet also spoke of the kingdom as still to come (e.g., Luke
11:2). Paul reflects this same dynamic, asserting that the 'end
of the ages' has come upon us (1 Cor. 10:11), but also looking
forward to a future consummation at the return of Christ
when all his enemies will be defeated and creation itself will
be transformed.

This reality radically changed Paul's understanding both of
the present and the future. Paul the Jew would have understood life in terms of this age and the age to come, with the
age to come following the conclusion of this age in chrono-
logical succession. For Paul the believer in Christ, the age to
come has broken into the present age, so that the two ages
overlap. Believers now live 'between the times', experiencing
the life and blessings of the age to come, but not yet as they
will one day experience them.

Paul's writings, then, while exhibiting significant continuity
with his past Jewish beliefs, demonstrate extraordinary
contrasts with them. The outpouring of the Spirit of the Lord,
understood as an end-time event in Judaism, has already taken
place (cf. Joel 2:28; Acts 2:1-21). The Spirit is present with the
church in a new and powerful way, enabling them to be
'witnesses' for Christ to the end of the earth (Acts 1:8).
Similarly for Paul, justification, an end-time declaration of
God in Judaism, is a present reality for those who have
trusted in Christ (cf. Rom. 5:1-11). In the light of his experience with Christ, Paul also began to understand the problem
of sin in a new way, as we shall see more clearly in the next
section.

The bottom line is that, while Paul certainly demonstrates
continuity with his Jewish past, his revelation that Christ had
come brought about profound contrasts as well. The Old

Testament remained foundational for him. But Paul began to distance himself from prevalent Jewish patterns of thought. After Damascus he read the Old Testament in the light of Christ, seeing Christ as the centre of history, the goal and the fulfilment of all of Israel's hopes. For Paul, the veil had been removed in his reading of the law; the light of the gospel had shone in his heart and life (2 Cor. 3:14 – 4:6).

3. Paul's encounter with the risen Christ led him to a new and more profound understanding of sin, especially of his own sinfulness

Whereas Paul could boast of his 'blameless' legal righteousness in Judaism (Phil. 3:6), he came to regard himself as the 'foremost', or 'chief' of sinners (1 Tim. 1:15). Ironically, Paul now recognized his own sinfulness precisely in the area where he would formerly have considered himself the most righteous, when his zeal for Judaism and the law led him to persecute those who in his view were perverting that law.

This is not to say that Paul saw his sin only in terms of zealous persecution or exclusivism. Though Paul elsewhere speaks of his sin of persecuting the church as making him undeserving of God's call to apostolic ministry (1 Cor. 15:9), the context of 1 Timothy 1 indicates that he sees his own sin more comprehensively. Not only was he a 'persecutor and a violent man' (NIV), but he was also a 'blasphemer' (1 Tim. 1:13) in his denial of Jesus as the Son of God. In short, Paul saw his sin as being that of unbelief (cf. 1 Tim. 1:13,16).

It is possible that in his own experience Paul did, as Sanders puts it, indeed move from solution to plight — the solution of Christ to the plight of human sin. Nevertheless the plight of human sin was not a creation of his own imagination, but a reflection on his and humanity's deeper problem, as well as on Old Testament Scriptures. Paul came to recognize the reality that 'none is righteous, no, not one' (Rom. 3:10), that all have sinned and fallen short of the glory of God

(Rom. 3:23). This sin problem is inherent in human nature (Eph. 2:3), and affects even well-meaning attempts to keep the law (Rom. 7:14-25). The formulations of the NPP continually downplay and de-emphasize the problem of sin that Paul so clearly and forcefully describes. When sin is discussed in the NPP, it is often defined in terms of community cohesion.

For Paul the primary problem with sin is not that everyone does it, nor is it the social and interpersonal effects of sin (though those exist). The primary problem, rather, is that sin has had disastrous consequences for humanity's relationship to God. Sin brings alienation from God and leads to condemnation. Paul says, 'The wrath of God is revealed from heaven against all ungodliness and unrighteousness of men' (Rom. 1:18). In fact, the key issue of Romans 1:18 – 3:20 is not so much that all humanity, both Jews and Gentiles, sin. It is, rather, the need to escape the righteous wrath of God poured out against human sin. In other words, the key question of the opening chapters of Romans, where Paul lays out his gospel (cf. Rom. 1:15-17), is 'How can sinners stand before a holy God?' Careful exegesis reveals that Paul's primary concern is exactly what proponents of the new perspective deny.

One of the ways the NPP has shifted the emphasis away from this central theme has been by arguing that Paul did not have a Luther-like guilty conscience prior to coming to faith in Christ. Certainly we do not see Paul agonizing over his sin and standing before God the way Luther did.[6] Paul declared that he was 'blameless' with regard to the righteousness under the law (Phil. 3:6). It is possible that he had the 'robust conscience' that Stendahl claims.[7] But the key issue is not an introspective, subjective, guilty conscience. It is rather objective guilt before God. For Paul, all are guilty because all have broken God's law. Whether plagued by guilt or not, all humanity stands before God's holy tribunal deserving his wrath and punishment. Paul himself came under conviction for his sin and repented of it.

The good news for Paul is that Jesus Christ 'loved me and gave himself for me' (Gal. 2:20). In Christ, God has dealt with the problem of sin to an extent far beyond what has been revealed in the Old Testament and taught in Judaism, though the shadows and types are clearly present there. Thus in Christ Paul discovered a new experience of God's grace.

4. On the Damascus Road, Paul came to know the grace of God truly for the first time

Without question, the Judaism of Paul's day taught, reflected on and basked in the grace of God in some sense. God chose the Jews, gave them his gracious revelation in the law and provided sacrifices for transgressions of the law. We appreciate the NPP's bringing this out so clearly. In fact, traditional Reformed theology has always taught that God's covenant with Israel was a continuation of the covenant of grace established with Abraham (cf. Gen. 15; Exod. 2:24).

But Paul consistently contrasts his own experience in Judaism, as well as that of his fellow Jews, with his new experience of grace in Christ. This is clear, for instance, in Galatians 2:19-21, where he seems to contrast his past experience under the law ('Through the law I died to the law,' v. 19) with his present experience of having been crucified with Christ, so that now Christ lives in him (v. 20). In the light of this, Paul asserts, 'I do not nullify the grace of God; for if justification were through the law, then Christ died for no purpose' (v. 21). The grace revealed in Christ far exceeds Paul's previous experience of grace in Judaism. Similarly, in Romans 11:6 he states, 'But if it is by grace, it is no longer on the basis of works; otherwise grace would no longer be grace.' It is possible even for those who speak of grace to turn grace into its opposite.

For Paul, the grace of the law is incomplete and insufficient without the grace revealed in Christ. Jews have the

benefit of the very oracles of God (Rom. 3:2). But a veil is
over their hearts when the old covenant is read (2 Cor.
3:12-16). Only when one turns to Christ is the veil removed
(2 Cor. 3:14,16). Jews as well as Gentiles, therefore, are
unbelievers whose minds have been blinded by the god of
this world (2 Cor. 4:4). This imagery of blinding was certainly
brought home powerfully for Paul when he was blinded on
the Damascus road. Now, for Paul, Christ Jesus has taken
hold of him and made him his own (Phil. 3:12), with the
result that Paul could certainly echo the refrain, 'Once I was
blind, but now I can see.'

Even in his zeal to uphold the law, Paul was a sinner.
Christ Jesus transformed him. This is the grace that Paul
speaks of so powerfully in his letters.

This leads to a final implication of Paul's encounter with
the risen Christ.

5. He came to recognize that justification does not come through rigorous law-observance

The classic passage supporting this is Philippians 3:7-9, where
Paul states his desire to 'be found in him, not having a righteousness of my own that comes from the law, but that which
comes through faith in Christ, the righteousness from God
that depends on faith' (v. 9). Dunn, however, argues against
understanding this passage as Paul's statement of righteousness as his own 'personal possession attained and defended by
personal effort'. According to Dunn, this interpretation
ignores the build-up to this statement in 3:4-6. He states:

> ... the confidence is not primarily, if at all, of per-
> sonal achievement. It is rather, once again, the con-
> fidence of Paul as a member of Israel, the covenant
> people — confident in his ethnic identity, confident in
> his share in the covenant marked by circumcision, con-
> fident that he was living within the terms of the coven-
> ant as laid out in the law, confident not least that he was

defending the distinctiveness of Israel and its separate-
ness from the nations, like zealous Phinehas and zealous Mattathias of old.[8]

Dunn's argument contains the seeds of its own demise. He
makes it clear that Paul did indeed set himself apart from
other Jews who were circumcised and part of the covenant
people in one sense. In fact, the very context of Philippians
3:1-6 indicates that Paul is comparing his own accomplishments with those of other Jews. Furthermore, his very persecution of other Jews indicates that he saw himself as righteous
because of his rigorous observance of the law, while other
Jews, who did not keep the law as he did, were not. The
bottom line for Paul, then, is not national, ethnic identity, but
who upholds the law of God. The larger national, covenantal
context is clearly present. But the key issue for Paul the Jew
was individual achievement within that larger context.

Paul clearly saw himself as part of a remnant within larger
ethnic, circumcised Israel. He explicitly makes the remnant
argument as a Christian in Romans 9 – 11 (cf. Rom. 9:6;
11:1-10). The difference is that, after the events of the Damascus Road, Paul understood the remnant in terms of faith
in Christ. Prior to that, he saw it in terms of rigorous law-
observance. His experience with the living Christ enabled
Paul to see that justification does not come through keeping
the law.

PAUL'S GOSPEL

Having looked at the impact of Paul's Damascus Road
experience on his life and theology, we now turn to look at
Paul's gospel. It is natural to assume that his gospel was
directly tied to his Damascus Road experience. His encounter
with the living Christ and his own personal faith in him would
certainly be central to his proclamation, the goal of which was

that others should know Christ and trust him for salvation. In fact, Paul sees his own experience of Christ Jesus reaching out to the 'chief of sinners' as an 'example', or 'pattern', of those who would put their faith in Christ (1 Tim. 1:16). In Galatians 1, Paul directly ties the reception of his gospel by 'a revelation of Jesus Christ' (1:12) to the revelation of God's Son in him (1:16) at his conversion.

Admittedly, Paul's teaching in his letters is tailored to the specific situations that he was addressing. He does not always use precisely the same language, and he often focuses on different aspects of his message. But when we look at Paul's letters to see the elements of his gospel and his brief summaries of his essential proclamation, we find a remarkable consistency. And we find that his gospel consistently reflects what we have already seen to have been his experience on the Damascus Road.

1. Paul's gospel proclaims salvation for sinners

Paul's writings contain several brief summary statements of what he preached, or of what he considered to be essential to the Christian message. These statements consistently reveal that at the heart of his message is God's provision of salvation for sinners. He states in 1 Timothy 1:15, 'The saying is trustworthy and deserving of full acceptance, that Christ Jesus came into the world to save sinners.' Saving sinners is, for him, the summation of Christ's life and ministry. In 1 Corinthians 15, Paul reminds the Corinthians of the gospel that he preached to them (v. 1). This gospel begins with the statement that 'Christ died for our sins in accordance with the Scriptures' (v. 3). Galatians begins with the similar summation that Christ 'gave himself for our sins' (Gal. 1:4).

As we have already seen, however, the key issue for Paul is not simply that human beings sin, nor that they have the status of 'sinners'. For him, the problem is the effect of their sin. That effect is twofold.

On the one hand, sinful human beings are deserving of the wrath of God (Rom. 1:18). As Paul says in the first part of Romans 6:23, 'the wages of sin is death'. Sinful human beings deserve death, God's judgement. But in Christ Jesus, God offers the free gift of eternal life (Rom. 6:23b).

On the other hand, those who sin 'fall short of the glory of God' (Rom. 3:23). The phrase 'the glory of God' refers to the glory that God created human beings to bear, a reflection of his own glory. Human sin has marred that glory. The good news is that those who are 'justified' in Christ will also be 'glorified' and 'conformed to the image' of the Son of God, Jesus Christ (Rom. 8:29-30).

Paul goes on in Romans 12 – 15 to make clear that there are significant corporate implications of this. In fact, he directly links Romans 8:29 to chapters 12 – 15 by the use of the same Greek root (*morph*) — 'being conformed [*summorphous*] to the image' of Christ (8:29) entails being 'transformed' (*metamorphousthe*) by the renewing of the mind (12:2). He then expounds this transformation in terms of body life in the chapters that follow. Believers show ongoing conformity to the image of Christ in loving one another, building up the body of Christ, and welcoming one another — especially those from different ethnic backgrounds — as Christ has welcomed them (Rom. 15:7).

The NPP emphasizes the corporate aspects in a way that obscures the personal and individual. In the NPP reading of Romans, the Jew/Gentile question is pre-eminent. For Paul, the body is composed of transformed individuals. It is important to recognize the order — forgiven and transformed individuals lead to forgiving and transformed communities. The NPP's emphasis on the corporate dimensions actually undercuts the building of ethnic unity that they rightly see in Paul.

To sum up, the good news of salvation in Christ begins with the bad news of human sin and guilt, which deserves the wrath and judgement of God. While Paul's experience in his encounter with Christ may have been from solution to plight, his own gospel and theological reflection have certainly moved from plight to solution. This should come as no surprise when we compare Paul's letters and his speeches in Acts to other early Christian preaching. John the Baptist's message is summarized as preaching a 'baptism of repentance for the forgiveness of sins' (Mark 1:4; Luke 3:3). He warned Jews to flee from the coming wrath (Luke 3:7). He preached the 'good news' (Luke 3:18) that God would gather the wheat into the barn, but that the chaff would be burned with unquenchable fire (Luke 3:17). The problem for Paul, reflecting the emphasis of the early church, was sin, and the solution for sin was a Saviour.

2. Paul's gospel proclaims the grace of God revealed in the life, death, resurrection and ascension of Jesus Christ

We saw in the previous section several gospel summaries that speak of Christ's death for sinners. We will speak more of that death shortly. But it is just as vital to see that, for Paul, Christ's death cannot be separated from his life, resurrection and ascension. In Romans 5, Paul contrasts the disobedience of Adam with the obedience of Christ, an obedience that N. T. Wright correctly argues refers not simply to his obedient death, but to his obedience throughout his life leading up to his death. Similarly, in Philippians 2, Paul asserts that Christ was obedient even 'to the point of death', an expression that refers to the extent of his obedience — faithful obedience that led even to obedience in death. The resurrection (e.g., 1 Cor. 15:4) and ascension (cf., e.g., Phil. 2:9-11; Rom. 8:34; Col. 3:1) are similarly central to Paul's proclamation, proclaiming Christ's victory over sin and death, and his rule over all the enemies of God.

But it is the death of Christ that Paul especially emphasizes. In 1 Corinthians 1:18, Paul refers to the 'message of the cross' (NIV) as 'the power of God,' which is similar to his description of the gospel as the 'power of God for salvation'

(Rom. 1:16). He goes on to tell the Corinthians that he determined to know nothing 'except Jesus Christ and him crucified' (1 Cor. 2:2). Paul's assertion to the Galatians that Christ 'loved me and gave himself for me' is in the context of his crucifixion (Gal. 2:20). We also need to see this in the light of the statement in Galatians 1:4, which we looked at earlier, that Christ 'gave himself for our sins'. In other words, Paul's summaries of his gospel continually refer to Christ's death.

The bigger question, however, is, what is the meaning of that death? First, *Christ's death provides atonement for sin*. Paul's references to the 'blood' of Christ (Rom. 3:25; 5:9; Eph. 1:7; 2:13; Col. 1:20) reflect the Old Testament motif of the blood of animals being offered as atonement for sin. Similarly, Paul's assertion that God sent his Son 'for sin' in Romans 8:3 could just as easily be translated 'as a sin offering' (as in NASB, NIV), since the Greek phrase is consistently used in the Septuagint (the Greek translation of the Hebrew Old Testament) to refer to the sin offering.

Secondly, *Christ's death is substitutionary*. When we combine Paul's statements that Christ died 'for our sins' (1 Cor. 15:3; Gal. 1:4) with his statements that Christ died 'for' us (Gal. 2:20; Rom. 5:6-8; 2 Cor. 5:15), it is logical to conclude that Christ died in our place, bearing the punishment that we deserved for our sins. This is confirmed by Galatians 3:13: 'Christ redeemed us from the curse of the law by becoming a curse for us.' We don't bear the curse of the law — namely, death; Christ did.

Thirdly, *Christ's death was propitiatory* — that is, it turned aside the wrath of God. We have already seen that in Romans 1:18 – 3:20 Paul focuses on the wrath of God poured out on human sin. In the light of this, Paul states in Romans 3:25 that God put Christ forward 'as a propitiation by his blood'. The death of Christ is the remedy for the just wrath of God against human sin. His blood satisfies that wrath because Christ himself has borne the brunt of it.

These Pauline emphases fly in the face of many new perspective writers, who at best de-emphasize substitutionary atonement and propitiation, and at worst deny them altogether. But they also once again highlight for us the key issue that new perspective writers undercut in Paul — namely, how can a sinner be justified in the light of the holy and just wrath of God? We can now say that the ground of that justification is the grace of God revealed in the work and merits of Jesus Christ. The instrument of that justification is faith.

3. Paul's gospel declares the good news that sinners are justified by faith alone, not by works (of the law)

One of the most glorious passages in all of Scripture is Romans 3:21-26. Here Paul brings together the themes looked at above of sin, grace and Christ's substitutionary, propitiatory death for sinners. But he also highlights the theme that will occupy him for the next chapter and a half — justification by faith, not by works of the law.

Paul begins this section by returning to the theme of Romans 1:17 — namely, 'the righteousness of God'. Over against Wright's assertion that God's righteousness is his covenant faithfulness, Romans 3:25-26 makes it clear that righteousness here refers to God's moral righteousness and/or his justice (the Greek word *dikaiosune* can mean 'justice'). We might expect Paul to say in verse 21 that, in spite of the bleak picture of human sin that he has just painted, yet now the *grace* of God has been revealed. Instead, he says God's righteousness has been revealed. How? God's 'passing over' of previously committed sin (v. 25) might make him appear to be unrighteous or unjust. As the holy and just Judge of the universe, God *must* punish sin. Yet God passed over sins because he planned all along to deal with them in the death of his Son.

While it is unjust for God not to punish sin, it is not unjust of God to punish sin vicariously. The reason God did this is so that his own people, those who put their faith in Christ and so are united to him, might not face his judgement. The opposite of judgement is justification. Thus Paul says that those who put their faith in Christ 'are justified by his grace as a gift, through the redemption that is in Christ Jesus' (v. 24). The result of this is that 'boasting' is excluded (v. 27) because no one, on account of their sin, can accomplish the works that gain favour with God — not even Abraham (Rom. 4:1-5).

Paul clearly here sets justification in the context of the believer's relationship with God. All have sinned; all deserve God's wrath; all have been cut off from God because of their sin. Yet, by faith in Christ and on the basis of his atoning work on the cross, sinners can be reconciled to God and declared to be in a right relationship with him (justified). Justification, then, highlights the vertical relationship between God and man. It is essential to the 'good news' of salvation.

The NPP, however, has moved justification out of the centre of Paul's thought and applied it more to the horizontal issue of ethnic unity than to the vertical relationship between God and man. Beginning with Stendahl, the move has been to see justification primarily in the light of Jew/Gentile relationships within the church. The most provocative and articulate of the NPP scholars to move and redefine justification has been N. T. Wright. He argues that 'the doctrine of justification by faith is not what Paul means by 'the gospel'',' although he does allow that justification is organically and integrally related to the gospel.[9] As we shall see in more detail in chapters 5-6, Wright understands justification primarily as the vindication of God's people over against their enemies. It is the declaration that someone belongs to the people of God and assures all who 'believe in Jesus' that they are part of the people of God. Justification thus identifies the true people of God and thereby also unites them.

According to Wright, justification provides the answer to 'the question of whether Jewish Christians were allowed to eat with Gentile Christians'.[10] He continues, 'Justification declares that all who believe in Jesus Christ belong at the same table, no matter what their cultural or racial differences.'[11] Thus justification is 'the great ecumenical doctrine'.[12]

We cannot do justice to Wright's argument here. But we can briefly respond to one argument in particular. Wright, with the rest of the NPP, is quick to point out that Paul's discussion of justification is largely confined to two letters, Romans and Galatians. Proponents of the NPP have drawn several conclusions from this, one being that justification is not central to Paul's thought. The other is a more carefully nuanced exegetical argument. As Wright puts it, '… virtually whenever Paul talks about justification he does so in the context of a critique of Judaism and of the coming together of Jew and Gentile in Christ.'[13] In other words, Romans and Galatians were largely written with the goal of ensuring ethnic unity in the church.

However, this assertion is not as 'blindingly obvious' as Wright believes. Galatians seems to be the best place to prove his argument because it clearly deals with Gentiles being forced to accept Jewish customs, particularly circumcision. But Paul does not treat the teaching of the 'agitators', as he calls them, as a matter of social impropriety. Neither does he address the Galatian Gentile believers in terms of exclusion from community involvement. Rather, salvation itself is at stake. He asks the Galatians, 'How did you receive the Spirit?' And he warns them that if they seek to be justified by the law, they will be severed from Christ (Gal. 5:4). Soteriology (the doctrine of salvation), not ecclesiology (the nature and structure of the church), is the pre-eminent concern in the letter.

Regarding Romans, Wright is certainly correct to read the letter in the light of Paul's mission to bring about 'the obedience of faith' among the nations (Rom. 1:5; 16:26), who are then engrafted into the Jewish root. We also see the coming together of Jew and Gentile in Paul's references to God's blessings coming 'to the Jew first and also to the Greek' (Rom. 1:16; 2:10), as well as chapters 14 – 15, in which both

Jew and Gentile are called to welcome one another, especially in the face of conflicts over food laws. Thus we can say that in one sense justification by faith is a unifying doctrine.

But, as we saw above in Romans 3:21-26, Paul places justification squarely in the context of God's work of redeeming sinners through the death of Christ and rescuing them from his just judgement. Justification is not, as Wright seems to argue, simply a declaration of what is already the case (namely, that one is 'in the right'). Rather, the declaration of justification makes a sinner legally innocent and puts him or her in a right relationship with God.

4. Paul's gospel proclaims a new, transformed humanity in Christ and looks forward to a new, transformed cosmos

All of this is not to say that Paul's gospel, which proclaims forgiveness of sin, justification by faith and reconciliation between God and man, is ahistorical or individualistic. According to Paul, God's intention is not simply to save souls, but to build a community of believers set apart for his glory. God is establishing 'one new man' (Eph. 2:15), bringing together Jewish and Gentile believers. This reconciliation brings him glory now and anticipates the day when people from every tribe and tongue and people and nation will worship before his throne. But the deliverance wrought in Christ will also bring about a redeemed cosmos (Rom. 8:18-22), which will be inhabited by believers living with transformed bodies. The problem of sin and alienation from God means both spiritual and physical death. God's solution in Christ means spiritual and physical life for evermore.

THE EVIDENCE FROM ACTS 13

Paul's speech in the synagogue in Pisidian Antioch in Acts 13:16-41 confirms the summation given above of his gospel based on his letters. The themes in this passage echo those which we have just detailed. Though Paul's original speech may have been longer, the record of it in Acts at least gives us what Luke deemed to be the essential elements of Paul's message. We, contrary to many proponents of the NPP, deem this speech to be a faithful rendering of Paul's original message. Significantly, this speech is delivered in the Roman province of Galatia. The gospel message that Paul proclaims here was the one that he called the Galatians back to in his letter to them.

In fact, there are significant parallels between Paul's speech in Acts 13 and his letter to the Galatians. Briefly, they are: the death of Christ (vv. 27-29), forgiveness of sins through Christ (v. 38), justification by faith, not through the law of Moses (vv. 38-39). Verses 38-39 are especially pertinent to our discussion: 'Through [Christ] ... everyone who believes [has faith] is justified from all things, from which you could not be justified through the law of Moses' (author's translation). In other words, the keeping of the law does not justify. Faith in Christ does justify. This is the heart of Paul's gospel, the good news that Jesus Christ saves sinners.

KEEPING FIRST THINGS FIRST

C. S. Lewis wrote:

> ... every preference of a small good to a great, or a partial good to total good, involves the loss of the small or partial good for which the sacrifice was made... You can't get second things by putting them first; you can get second things only by putting first things first.

The NPP has put a dangerous emphasis on second things that threatens, if not abolishes, first things.

The desire for unity among Christians is a good and admirable one. We are in substantial agreement with Wright's basic premise that God's plan from the very beginning was to make one single family from all nations on earth. But, as we shall see in more detail in chapter 5, Wright's formulations undercut the foundation for that unity. We maintain that Wright, though differing in his formulation, stands with the rest of the NPP in putting second things first. When that happens, you lose both first and second things. You get second things only by putting first things first.

In Paul's teaching, what are those first things? Of first importance to Paul is the answer to the question, 'How can sinners stand before a just and holy God?' The answer: 'By God's grace alone, on the basis on Christ's life, death, resurrection and ascension, and received by faith alone.' When we agree on these things, we are freed to live in love and unity, for the glory of God and the advance of his kingdom.

3.

WAS PAUL BATTLING AGAINST JEWISH LEGALISM?

The driving force of the NPP has been Sanders' conclusion that first-century Judaism was not a religion of legalistic works-righteousness, in which Jews sought to earn favour with God by their good works. This is a significant assertion because Paul consistently sets his doctrine of justification by faith over against 'works', or 'works of the law', traditionally seen in Reformation circles as human attempts to earn God's favour by one's deeds. According to Sanders, this view arose because the Reformers viewed first-century Judaism through the lens of medieval Catholicism. By contrast, he argues that first-century Judaism was a religion of grace. The older view, treating Paul's gospel as a response to Jewish legalism, was therefore rooted in a fundamental misunderstanding of Judaism, and so was a misreading of Paul.

Sanders' work was foundational for the leading proponents of the NPP, especially Dunn and Wright. Wright has consistently asserted that Sanders' basic conclusion has been established,[1] and he chides New Testament interpreters for reading Paul in the light of a Judaism that did not exist.[2] James Dunn has come to the same conclusions with regard to Sanders' work. Both call for a new reading of Paul in the light of Sanders' detailed study. It is important, then, that we take some time to examine Sanders' thesis. The basic question is: was Paul battling against first-century Jewish legalism? We will answer in the affirmative by arguing, firstly, that first-century Judaism was more complex than Sanders indicates; secondly, that first-century Judaism was legalistic even on the basis of Sanders' own description of it; thirdly, that Jesus' words confirm the presence of legalism; and, fourthly, that Paul's letters give clear evidence of his battle against Jewish and Jewish-Christian legalism.

SANDERS' THESIS ON FIRST-CENTURY PALESTINIAN JUDAISM

'The Sanders revolution', as some have called it, was set off by the publication of E. P. Sanders' book, *Paul and Palestinian Judaism*, in 1977. In many ways, this volume is a wonderfully learned and informative study of first-century Judaism. As Sanders methodically works through the various writings of the time, he detects a consistent 'pattern of religion'. A 'pattern of religion,' on his terms, refers to how a religion's adherents understand the process of 'getting in and staying in'.[3] According to Sanders, the pattern of religion found in Jewish writings indicated to him that first-century Judaism was not a religion of legalistic works-righteousness. Rather, it was a religion of grace.

In particular, Sanders described first-century Judaism's pattern of religion as that of 'covenantal nomism'. We can break that term down into its two parts. 'Covenantal' refers, of course, to the covenant that the sovereign God, by his own initiative, has made with Israel. He has entered into a relationship with them in which he becomes their God and they become his people. The term 'nomism' is based on the Greek word *nomos*, which means 'law'.

According to covenantal nomism, one becomes a member of the community by God's electing grace. Jews belong to God and are 'saved' because they are part of the covenant that God has graciously made with them. Jews keep the law, then, for two reasons. First, they obey the law in thankful response to God's covenant and out of love for God. Secondly, they keep the law to maintain their membership within the covenant community. In Sanders' terms, then, the Jews believed that they 'entered' the covenant by grace, but that they 'maintained' their standing in the covenant by works — that is, by obedience to the law.

Even with regard to obedience, however, we still see God's grace at work since God has provided sacrifices to deal with sin. Perfect obedience, then, is not required. What is required is the intent to obey and the commitment to remain within the covenant.[4] The following statement regarding the teachings of the rabbis sums up Sanders' understanding of the general outlook of first-century Judaism:

> The all-pervasive view is this: all Israelites have a share in the world to come unless they renounce it by renouncing God and his covenant. All sins, no matter of what gravity, which are committed within the covenant, may be forgiven as long as a man indicates his basic intention to keep the covenant by atoning, especially by repenting of transgression.[5]

RESPONSE TO SANDERS

In response to Sanders, we can say that in one sense he has succeeded in his task. He states that one of his chief aims in the book is 'to destroy the view of Rabbinic Judaism which is still prevalent in much, perhaps most, New Testament scholarship'.[6] In particular, the view that he seeks to destroy is the belief 'that Judaism is a religion in which one must *earn* salvation by compiling more good works ("merits"), whether on his own or from the excess of someone else, than he has transgressions'.[7] In other words, Sanders sees his sparring partners as being those who hold to the view that first-century Judaism consisted of a crass system of weighing merits over against demerits. To this we cry 'no contest' and throw in the towel. In fact, we ourselves have never viewed Judaism in that way and so would not even want to enter the ring on that issue. Without a doubt, Sanders has won that fight.

However, there are more significant issues that remain. We will raise two questions about Sanders' work (these also apply, of course, to those who adopt his conclusions). The first is the question of whether 'covenantal nomism' is an adequate overall description of first-century Judaism. Sanders himself admits that there are exceptions to the pattern that he has detected. There is even some crass weighing of merits and demerits! (More on this later.) So this issue demands further scrutiny. The second question is, even if Sanders is right, does his notion of 'covenantal nomism' exclude legalism? To these we now turn.

1. Is 'covenantal nomism' an adequate description of first-century Judaism?

It is important to understand the context and scope of Sanders' study. As the title of his book suggests, his research was limited to an examination of the writings that emerged out of 'Palestinian' Judaism — that is, Jews living in Palestine, or Israel — between 200 BC and AD 200. His study did not include, for instance, the writings of first-century Jews like Philo, who lived in Alexandria. This observation is not meant as a criticism of Sanders. All studies need limits. But we do need to understand the scope of his examination.

More important is Sanders' conclusion that the 'consistent' outlook in Palestinian Jewish writings means that 'covenantal nomism' was the 'pervasive' pattern of religion, and so the type of Judaism known to Jesus and Paul.[8] This may be a correct assumption. It may not be. Paul, of course, was a Hellenistic Jew, who was born in Tarsus in Asia Minor, though he did train in Jerusalem. Sanders admits that we

know very little of the Judaism of Asia Minor. Our point here
is simply that one should be cautious about coming to dra-
matically new interpretations of Paul based on a fairly limited
reading of Judaism. Others since Sanders have attempted to
fill in some of the gaps left by his work.[9] But the fact remains
that the 'Sanders revolution' had taken off long before all of
the pertinent evidence was in.

In fact, recent studies have called into question whether
the first-century Jewish pattern of religion was as consistent
as Sanders and his followers claim it to be. The most comprehensive study since Sanders' original work is the recent
book, *Justification and Variegated Nomism, Volume 1: The Complexities of Second Temple Judaism*, edited by D. A. Carson, Peter
O'Brien and Mark Seifrid.[10] This work is greater in its scope
and more comprehensive than Sanders' study. In many ways,
it confirms the pattern of covenantal nomism that Sanders
had earlier found in his study of Palestinian Judaism. But, as
the title suggests, the various essays make clear that Second
Temple Judaism is too complex to be summed up using the
description 'covenantal nomism'. The literature does not all fit
neatly into Sanders' pattern. In other words, the Jewish
writings do not clearly indicate that 'getting in' is by grace, but
'staying in' is by obedience to the law; nor are these two sides
adequately held in balance.

For example, Robert Kugler's treatment of the *Testament of
Moses* demonstrates that the writer believed Israel to be both
elected by grace and kept by grace.[11] Although Israel may sin,
God 'will be faithful to his covenant and oath to sustain the
people...'[12] Kugler concludes by asserting that the *Testament*
meets Sanders' criteria 'half-way': '... the *Testament* does
understand Israel to have been elected by God, but it seems
to preclude the possibility that Israel could "unelect" itself by
a failure to keep the law.'[13]

The biggest problem, however, is the plethora of writings
in which grace takes a back seat or is absent altogether.

In some Jewish writings, *God's grace is marginalized* with regard to 'entering' the covenant, such as in the story of *Joseph and Aseneth*.[14] As Craig Evans points out, this story presupposes God's choice and election of Israel.[15] But Aseneth's conversion and ultimate immortality are the result of her repentance, as well as her change in lifestyle and diet by adopting Jewish food and purity laws. Likewise, God's pardoning of Adam and Eve (*Life of Adam and Eve*) and their entrance into the 'paradise of heaven' was 'not entirely the result of God's grace; it was in response to their vigorous penance'.[16]

In other writings, there is *little emphasis on God's grace in election,* with the stress placed upon works and merits for staying in. Sanders himself notes that 1 Enoch is 'notably defective' because it lacks some important gracious elements of the covenant, though he argues that these elements are 'presupposed'.[17] But these elements are absent in many other Jewish writings as well.[18]

All of this is complicated by two other factors. The first is that the Jews who are addressed in the literature are *in the covenant by birth*. Thus, Peter Enns asks the question whether it is appropriate to speak of 'getting in' at all.[19] The second is that some of the literature, such as that produced by the Qumran community, manifestly arises from *a community that the members have to join* to be part of. While some of the Qumran literature does hold out hope for some who are within larger Israel, 'remnant' language is prominent, as is the idea that atonement is strictly for members of the sect. Either way, Markus Bockmuehl concludes that the teaching of the Qumran community on salvation was in 'flux', and not a 'monolithic theological construct'.[20]

In still other writings, God's grace in election is strongly present, but equally highlighted, if not more so, is the theme of *human works as guaranteeing future salvation and justification*. The book of IV Ezra, written in response to the fall of Jerusalem in AD 70, seems to be an example of this. Interestingly,

Sanders himself saw IV Ezra as an exception to the pattern of
covenantal nomism, arguing that there 'judgement *is* strictly
according to deeds', and not on the basis of God's mercy.[21]
But Richard Bauckham's assessment is more accurate in
recognizing that the theme of mercy is present in IV Ezra,
particularly with regard to the grace of God in choosing Israel
and entering into covenant with her. This leads Bauckham to
conclude that in IV Ezra, salvation for the righteous is 'both a
matter of reward, within the terms God has given, but also a
matter of God's grace, in that he freely chose to make such a
covenant with Israel'.[22]

This last pattern, in which salvation is the result of both
grace and merit, appears to be a prominently recurring theme
in the Jewish writings.[23]

These examples are enough to cause us to wonder whether
'covenantal nomism' is an adequate description of the Judaism of Paul's day. As D. A. Carson has put it, the expression
'covenantal nomism' is both reductionistic and misleading. It
gives the impression that there is more uniformity in Judaism
than there really is.[24]

Perhaps part of the problem with Sanders' work is a
methodological one — that is, one dealing with his approach
to the Jewish literature. Twenty-five years ago, soon after
Sanders' work appeared, Jacob Neusner, a man who has
devoted his life to studying the Jewish literature, accused *Paul
and Palestinian Judaism* of being methodologically flawed.
Sanders' method amounted to coming at Judaism from the
perspective of questions raised by reading Paul and his
interpreters (and a misreading of Paul at that, we might add).
The result, according to Neusner, is that Sanders has imposed
artificial categories that are not native to the texts.[25] The
wisdom of this evaluation has been confirmed by recent
studies. But, more importantly, it calls into question whether
first-century Judaism was really as consistent as Sanders
claims. When you impose categories from the outside, there is
the obvious tendency to try to make the pieces 'fit'.

In any case, it does not appear that a catch-all description like 'covenantal nomism' can adequately convey the diversity in the Jewish literature.

Our brief survey above reveals another, possibly more significant, problem. Though grace is clearly present in Jewish thinking and writing, so is merit. In fact, the way that works and merit are highlighted calls into question whether salvation really is by grace, as Sanders asserts. In fact, Richard Bauckham points out that:

> The very basic and flexible pattern of covenantal nomism [can] take forms in which the emphasis is overwhelmingly on meriting salvation by works of obedience to the Law, with the result that human achievement takes center-stage and God's grace, while presupposed, is effectively marginalized.[26]

D. A. Carson succinctly says that Sanders' construct of covenantal nomism 'includes and baptizes a great deal of merit theology'.[27]

We now turn to a closer examination of this insight.

2. Does 'covenantal nomism' exclude legalism?

The prominent place of works and merit in Judaism raises the question, even if 'covenantal nomism' were an accurate description of first-century Judaism (though that is open to debate), does this mean that legalism is thereby excluded? Our answer to this is 'No'. Sanders' definition of legalism is a narrow one. By other standards of what constitutes legalism (including that of the Reformation tradition), even many Jewish writings that do indeed fit the 'covenantal nomism' pattern can still be characterized as legalistic. In other words, they teach that even when God's grace is present, final salvation is ultimately the result of works and merit.

In fact, there are numerous hints and admissions on Sanders' part that point to legalism, at the same time as he and others deny its presence. As Stephen Westerholm puts it, while Sanders' 'slogans' have been adopted by NPP advocates, 'it is worth asking whether subtleties in his text have been missed'.[28] For instance, Sanders asserts that for Jewish rabbis 'grace and merit did not seem ... to be in contradiction to each other'.[29] He goes on to say that Palestinian Judaism did not consider 'grace and works [to be] alternate roads to salvation'.[30] If that is true, can we legitimately say, with Sanders, that in Judaism 'salvation is always by the grace of God'?[31] Merit, by Sanders' own description, also plays a part.

In addition, Sanders admits that the rabbis found merit even in God's choosing of Israel. While they affirmed God's gracious election, they regarded God as 'reasonable', and concluded that he must therefore have a reason for his election of Israel. So they asked, 'Why did God choose the Jews?' The answers, Sanders reports, include the following: God offered the covenant to all, but only Israel accepted it; God chose Israel because of some merit found either in the patriarchs or in the Exodus generation, or on the condition of future obedience.[32] For at least some Jews, then, merit is required for 'getting in' after all. Does this not open the door to all kinds of legalism? These answers are certainly a far cry from the biblical record as found in 1 Corinthians 1:26-28, or even Deuteronomy 7:7-8.

Sanders also points out that rabbinic literature even speaks of salvation depending on God's weighing good deeds against bad in the Day of Judgement. But, Sanders asserts, such statements are there only for homiletic or 'exhortative' purposes.[33] They do not truly reflect the rabbis' view of salvation. Yet we are left to wonder where we can draw the line between what is preached and what is believed. Furthermore, which did the 'people in the pews' take to heart?

All of this seriously damages the claim that legalism is absent in first-century Judaism.

It is clear, in fact, that many Jewish writings portray works and merit as being conditions for salvation. In spite of the presence of God's grace, when works and merit are seen as instrumental in salvation, we have legalism. Peter Enns, for example, at the end of a study of Jewish 'expansions' of Scripture in which he largely agrees with Sanders about the presence of a pattern of covenantal nomism, asks the question, 'Is salvation the best word to describe one's *initiation* into the covenant wholly apart from the final outcome?'[34] He goes on to state, 'It might be less confusing to say that *election* is by grace but *salvation* is by obedience.' The bottom line is that, in many Jewish writings, some more than others, salvation is the result of grace plus works.

We need to remember that Sanders is out to 'destroy' the view that first-century Judaism sees salvation as a matter of totting up merits and demerits. As we have indicated, he is largely correct on that score — even though this totting up is present! But the weighing of merits and demerits is only one form of legalism. Has Sanders shown that legalism is not present in Judaism? Hardly. On the contrary, he has made a strong case for its presence.

A ROSE BY ANY OTHER NAME ... STILL SMELLS LIKE LEGALISM!

The leading proponents of the NPP, Dunn and Wright, both of whom profess to be Bible-believing Christians (Wright also claims to be Reformed), root their reinterpretation of Paul in Sanders' reconstruction. Although many of their interpretations of individual passages would hold up apart from their particular understanding of first-century Judaism, it is clear that were the historical foundation to crumble, so would their innovative reading of Paul. The next three chapters will deal more directly with Dunn (chapter 4) and Wright (chapters 5-6), and their reinterpretation of Paul. But in view of what we have seen above, we need to look more closely at some of the statements that Dunn and Wright make regarding first-century Judaism.

In the light of Sanders' findings, Dunn declares, 'Judaism is first and foremost a religion of grace, with human obedience always understood as response to that grace.'[35] Correspondingly, Dunn asserts, '"covenantal nomism" is remarkably like the classic Reformation theology of works — that good works are the consequence and outworking of divine grace, not the means by which that grace is first attained'. Jews, therefore, preached 'good Protestant doctrine' all along.[36]

But the covenantal nomism that we have seen above is a long way from the theology of the Reformers. Clearly, many of the Jewish writings understand works as instrumental in salvation or as the ground of salvation, not simply as the response or evidence of saving faith, as in classic Protestant theology.

Dunn's review of *Justification and Variegated Nomism, Volume 1*, is illuminating with regard to his overall outlook.[37] He happily regards the essays as affirming Sanders' pattern of covenantal nomism. He takes D. A. Carson's concluding essay to task for questioning the legitimacy of the term 'covenantal nomism', suggesting that he and Carson seem to have read different essays. But what Dunn fails to see is that the crucial issue is not so much whether a pattern of covenantal nomism can be detected, as it is whether legalism has been excluded. In fact, Dunn fails to interact with the question of whether merit theology was present in the Jewish literature, even though the issue constantly appears throughout the book. For Dunn, evidently, a theology of grace plus works leading to acceptance with God is simply good, gracious doctrine.

N. T. Wright insists that first-century Judaism was not 'a religion of legalistic works-righteousness'.[38] But how he goes on to describe this is telling. Judaism was not, he says, a form of 'Pelagianism, according to which humans must pull themselves up by their moral bootstraps and thereby earn justification…'[39] For Wright, in other words, 'legalism' amounts to 'Pelagianism'.

Wright, however, fails to see that the key issue is not Pelagianism, but semi-Pelagianism. Pelagianism was an ancient heresy that taught that, because human nature was not corrupted by Adam's fall (Adam had simply set a bad example), individuals could be saved on the basis of their own free will and moral effort alone. They did not need God's grace except in the sense that it was God who gave them free will and provided his moral law to guide them. We agree that, at least on the basis of the literature, few Jews of Paul's day seem to have held to this position. But semi-Pelagianism is another issue.

Semi-Pelagianism does not deny human sinfulness and the need for God's transforming grace. In fact, it proclaims that salvation is initially prompted by God's grace. But in semi-Pelagianism, human works cooperate with God's grace to merit more grace and ultimately salvation. In effect, then, semi-Pelagianism proclaims a gospel of grace plus works leading to salvation and acceptance with God.

The Reformers did not oppose medieval Catholicism's view of justification because it was Pelagian. Rather, they opposed its semi-Pelagianism — salvation based on God's grace and human cooperation with that grace. Ultimately, they viewed semi-Pelagianism as legalism. This is precisely the type of teaching that Paul opposed and it is directly in conflict with his gospel of grace alone.

The key question then is not, 'Was first-century Judaism a form of Pelagianism?' Rather it is, 'Was first-century Judaism semi-Pelagian?' The broad category that Sanders dubs 'covenantal nomism' clearly includes within it many forms of semi-Pelagianism. As Cornel Venema puts it, 'Sanders' description of "covenantal nomism" closely resembles a kind of text-book description of semi-Pelagian teaching and therefore lends unwitting support to the Reformation argument.'[40]

In this light, viewed from the perspective of theological foundations, first-century Judaism in some respects begins to look like medieval Catholicism, and the teaching of the

Reformers lines up closely with that of the apostle Paul. Both were opposing a teaching that insisted on salvation by grace plus works — that is, legalism. Legalism is the enemy of the gospel. The antidote is the true gospel of grace alone through faith alone in Christ alone.

THE NEW TESTAMENT EVIDENCE OF JEWISH LEGALISM

1. The evidence from Jesus and the Gospels

If first-century Jews had the law/grace balance right, we would expect words of commendation, not criticism, from the lips of Jesus. In fact, what we find is just the opposite. Pharisees in particular, beloved and followed by Jews of their own day and the source for the later compilation of writings known as the 'rabbinic literature', come under fire by Jesus. The Pharisees, Jesus says, were concerned about the minutiae of the law and neglected the weightier matters (Matt. 23:23-24). They were focused on externals to the neglect of the heart (Matt. 23:25-28). They failed to see that the law speaks not just to external deeds, but also to sins of the heart (Matt. 5:17-48) — in part, to reveal the stringency of God's demands and the inability to live up to that standard (cf. Matt. 5:48). Nicodemus, a prominent Pharisee ('the teacher of Israel,' John 3:10) did not understand the necessity of spiritual rebirth. The Jewish leaders failed to see that they were in bondage to sin (John 8:31-47) and could be set free only by faith in the Son of God.

In short, the most prominent Jewish leaders in Jesus' day were consumed by external performance as a means to acceptance by God and man. They had misunderstood their own law, which was meant to point them to Christ (John 5:39-47). Although the law was indeed God's gracious gift to Israel, they had perverted that grace and turned it into its opposite.

Sanders makes a comment with regard to Jesus and the Gospels that is quite telling. He states, 'The possibility cannot be completely excluded that there were Jews accurately hit by the polemic of Matt. 23... One must say, however, that the surviving Jewish literature does not reveal them.'[41] Do we accept the testimony of the only begotten Son of God, the searcher of hearts, who was incarnate and actually lived in first-century Palestine? Or should we trust the reconstruction of a twentieth-century historian, piecing the evidence together from scattered literature that at best leads to inconsistent conclusions? Christians who base their life and faith on the Word of God must accept the testimony of their Lord.

The bottom line is that Sanders and his colleagues have painted a rosy picture of the first-century Jewish teachers that directly contradicts the one portrayed by Jesus. To paraphrase Sanders, the possibility cannot be completely excluded that there were Jews who had an accurate understanding of the relationship between law and grace (indeed, we believe there were true believers among the Jews). One must say, however, that, by Jesus' own testimony, they are not prominent.

2. The evidence from Paul

The most important evidence that Paul was battling against Jewish legalism comes from Paul himself. We will look briefly at a few key passages that clearly indicate the presence, at least from Paul's perspective, of legalism. We will only look at this issue briefly here because we will return to it in the next chapter when we examine James Dunn's interpretation of the Pauline phrase 'works of the law'. In chapter 4, for example, we will look more closely at key passages from Galatians. Outside of Galatians, three passages in particular point to the presence of legalism among Jews.

Romans 3:27 – 4:8

Romans is a good place to begin because it does not have the same polemical edge that, for instance, Galatians does. In Galatians, Paul is addressing the problem of false teachers and clearly goes on the attack (cf., e.g., Gal. 1:6-10; 3:1). In Romans, while Paul addresses specific issues and problems in the church (as in all his other letters), he is writing, at least in part, to introduce himself and his gospel to the Roman Christians. Thus he writes in careful, measured tones.

In the section leading up to Romans 3:27 – 4:8, Paul has laid out the bad news of human sin (1:18 – 3:20) and the good news of salvation in Christ (3:21-26). Justification, Paul writes, is a gift of God's grace (v. 24) — a glorious example of redundant language! — achieved through Christ's atoning, propitiating death (vv. 24-25) and received by faith (vv. 25-26). If justification is all of God and is given in spite of human sin, then the corollary is obvious — it does not come through works that human beings do.

This is the basis for Paul's question in Romans 3:27 (as confirmed by the word 'therefore', or 'then'): 'Where then is boasting?' (NASB). This question seems to carry two connotations, both of which are confirmed in the discussion that follows. The first is that Jews actually were boasting, or at least seeking a reason to boast. The second is that they were seeking a reason to boast in their own works as a result of earning favour with God. But Paul's point is that no one has a boast before God, because no one can earn God's favour. Salvation is God's gracious gift. Sin nullifies the possibility of human merit.

Paul's question, 'Where ... is boasting?', in Romans 3:27 needs to be seen in the light of his references to boasting in the previous chapter and in Romans 4:2. In chapter 2, Paul has already referred to Jewish boasting ('in God', v. 17; 'in the law', v. 23). The implication of the return to the subject of boasting in chapter 3, then, is that this boasting also is something that the Jews were engaged in.[42] The fact that Paul goes on in chapter 4 to elaborate on this theme, specifically discussing whether in fact Abraham, 'our forefather', had a reason to boast, would also seem to confirm that he is battling against boasting in some form. It is only logical that Paul goes to such great lengths in discussing this question because it is something that he perceives to be a present problem.

Furthermore, Paul's refutation of boasting is directed against the ability to boast in one's works. In Romans 3:27, he says that boasting is excluded not by a law of works, but by a law of faith. The implication is that boasting would be legitimate if one were able to be justified by one's works. Two specific statements in chapter 4 confirm this interpretation.

First, Paul states in verse 2, 'For if Abraham was justified by works, he has something to boast about, but not before God.' At first glance, this statement is awkward. Does Abraham have something to boast about, or does he not? How can he both have a reason to boast and not have a reason to boast? Is Paul saying that Abraham does have a reason to boast before men, but not before God? No, the context for this statement is justification, or one's standing with God. What accounts, then, for the awkwardness of Paul's statement?

It is likely that Paul is dealing with a Jewish understanding in the first century that held to an exalted view of Abraham's righteousness. In one writing, for instance, it is said that 'Abraham was perfect in all his deeds with the Lord, and well-pleasing in righteousness all the days of his life' (Jubilees 23:10).[43] Similarly, 1 Maccabees 2:52 says, 'Was not Abraham found faithful in temptation, and it was reckoned unto him for righteousness?' Paul, for the sake of argument, for a split second leaves open the possibility that Abraham was righteous because of his deeds and therefore can boast, only to turn around and flatly deny it ('but not before God'). This gives us a glimpse into the fact that the Jews of Paul's day (as well as today) had a more optimistic view of human ability to obey than Paul did (more on this in the next chapter). But it is also clear proof that Paul is linking 'boasting' with achieving one's own justification by works.

Secondly, Paul is unambiguous in verses 4-5 that he is refuting the idea that one's own works merit salvation: 'Now to the one who works, his wages are not counted as a gift but as his due. And to the one who does not work but trusts him who justifies the ungodly, his faith is counted as righteousness.' The contrast is clearly between what is owed as a just reward to someone who works and what is given as a gift. Thus the refutation of justification by works is a refutation of justification by human merit. The gift of righteousness, on the other hand, includes both the imputation, not earning, of righteousness (vv. 3,5,6,9) and the forgiveness of sins (vv. 6-8). Furthermore, this gift of righteousness can only be received by faith (vv. 3,5,9).

Sanders and Dunn[44] argue that Paul here is opposing privileged status, not meritorious obedience. In other words, Paul is combating Jewish exclusivity and nationalism, boasting in their status over against Gentiles. Sanders, for example, argues that the earlier references to 'boasting' in chapter 2 refer to boasting in status, and so it is logical that 'boasting' in Romans 3 – 4 should have the same meaning. Furthermore, both Sanders and Dunn appeal to Romans 3:29-30 — that God is not the God of the Jews only, but also of the Gentiles — to support this position.

We agree that Paul opposes Jewish boasting over Gentiles. Both, he has asserted, have sinned and deserve God's wrath, and so Jews cannot claim special privilege. In fact, the best of the 'old perspective' interpreters have recognized that part of Paul's purpose in Romans 2 – 4 is to attack the notion that Jews had a special status over Gentiles.[45] The problem with the NPP is that that is all they see.

The appeal to Abraham in Romans 4:2 and the references to works deserving wages in verses 4-5 point to legalism, not nationalism, as Paul's primary target.[46] The appeal to God's being the God of both Jews and Gentiles is simply further support for Paul's position. If justification were through works of the Mosaic law, then salvation would have been for Jews only, the recipients of that law. But the fact that God is God of the Gentiles is another indication that justification is by God's grace alone through faith alone.

In short, Paul is battling against a perceived Jewish legalism in which works (typically in cooperation with God's grace) merited God's favour leading to justification. In place of this, Paul asserts his gospel of justification by grace alone through faith alone in Christ alone. This, of course, is the interpretation that has been predominant in the Reformation tradition for almost five hundred years, and it still stands as the best and most logical reading of the text.

Romans 9:30 – 10:8

This passage from later in Romans confirms our interpretation given above that Paul was opposing Jewish legalism. He begins by saying that Gentiles have achieved the righteousness that Jews pursued, but did not attain. Then, in verse 32, he asks the question, 'Why?' The answer: 'Because they did not pursue it by faith, but as if it were based on works.'

Notice two things about this passage. First, Israel pursued (literally) the 'law of righteousness', most likely meaning the 'law that would lead to righteousness'. In other words, righteousness was not something they already had by being part of the covenant people. Rather, they pursued righteousness so as to attain it. But, secondly, they pursued it in the wrong way — not by faith, but as though it could be attained by works.[47] In other words, by their works they attempted to earn their salvation.

Paul says something similar in Romans 10:3, when he asserts that the Jews did not submit to God's righteousness, but sought to establish 'their own'. This has traditionally, and rightly, been understood as legalism.

Dunn, on the other hand, understands this verse to be a reference to the Jews understanding 'the law defining righteousness ... too narrowly in terms of the requirements of the law which mark off Jew from Gentile'.[48] He goes on to say:

> Israel's mistake was not that they had understood righteousness as obedience to the law ... but that they had understood obedience to the law too much in terms of specific acts of obedience like circumcision, sabbath observance, and ritual purity ... they had treated the law and the righteousness it requires at too superficial and too nationalistic a level...[49]

He understands 'their own righteousness' in 10:3 to refer not to their own efforts to achieve righteousness before God, but as resting in the status peculiar to them as Jews, to the exclusion of Gentiles.

The problem with this interpretation is twofold. First, 'God's righteousness', or 'the righteousness from God', is mentioned twice in this verse, and it is put in clear contrast to 'their own'. The natural reading, then, is a contrast between the righteousness that God gives and that which the Jews were attempting to attain. In other words, the contrast is not Jewish righteousness against the Gentiles; it is their own righteousness over against God's. Secondly, Paul goes on to describe the 'righteousness that is based on the law' (10:5) in terms of well-meaning, but vain activity — ascending into heaven (10:6), descending into the abyss (10:7). The Jews were pursuing righteousness through activity that was in itself good (obedience to the law), but when used as a means to a right standing with God is legalism.

Philippians 3:2-11

This passage provides an important parallel to what we have just seen in Romans 10. In language that calls to mind the Jews' pursuit of 'their own' righteousness, Paul contrasts 'a righteousness of my own that comes from the law' with 'that which comes through faith in Christ, the righteousness from God that depends on faith' (v. 9). Here, Paul speaks in very personal terms of his own reasons to put confidence in the flesh (vv. 3-4). These include his status as a Jew, but focus mostly on his zeal and righteousness under the law (he has more reason for confidence in the flesh than others). This is legalism, seeking a reason for boasting in one's accomplishments and establishing a claim on God's acceptance.

The contrast with Paul's own righteousness is 'the righteousness from God', that which God gives and God alone can provide. The implication is that Paul is setting out a contrast between the righteousness that is a gift from God and the righteousness that an individual seeks to attain. The proper response to God's righteousness is faith (repeated twice in v. 9). Faith, at the root of which is the notion of trust, means receiving and resting in the righteousness that God provides. As such, it is the antithesis of legalism. Once again, then, as we have seen earlier, the contrast is between one's effort to achieve one's own righteousness and resting in the righteousness that God has provided.

Dunn argues, similarly to what we have already seen, that Paul is not combating legalism here, but Jewish nationalism. He is criticizing the efforts of Jews to establish their own covenantal righteousness over against the Gentiles.[50] But there are three problems with Dunn's interpretation.

The first is the very personal nature of Paul's argument. He speaks of his own righteousness, not some kind of nationalistic righteousness of the Jews in relation to Gentiles.

Secondly, Paul here is pitting his own righteousness over against other Jews — not Gentiles. The most natural interpretation of verses 2-3 is that Paul is opposing Judaizers, those Jewish Christians who were trying to compel Gentiles to be circumcised. Paul, then, is citing reasons for his ability to boast in his own accomplishments in Judaism in comparison with theirs ('if anyone ... thinks he has reason for confidence in the flesh, I have more').

Thirdly, Dunn's interpretation rests heavily on the idea of 'boundary markers', such as circumcision, food laws and Sabbath observance, which distinguish Jews from Gentiles. But Paul's list of accomplishments in verses 4-6, while including his status as a Jew, goes far beyond mere boundary markers.

Sanders, on the other hand, argues that Paul is speaking positively of life under Judaism because he refers to this life as a 'gain'. Paul is, therefore, not finding fault with his former legalistic effort to attain righteousness.[51] At the same time, the fact that Paul was 'blameless' under the law indicates, according to Sanders, that his problem with life under the law was not inability to carry out its requirements.[52] Instead, Paul rejects life under the law because of a salvation-historical shift — God's plan for salvation has turned a corner with the coming of Christ. Now salvation is available only in Jesus Christ.[53]

We agree with Sanders that *one* of Paul's arguments throughout his letters is that there has been a salvation-historical shift. But Paul speaks of his life in Judaism as being 'gain' even after that shift has taken place. It does not matter whether we conceive of the shift as taking place with the birth, life, death, resurrection or ascension of Christ, since Paul's persecution of the church (v. 6) was clearly after all of these things. But by Sanders' own reckoning, life in Judaism was not a 'gain', in Paul's view, since this shift. Paul, then, must be speaking of a *perceived* gain in Judaism. He had previously perceived of his life in Judaism as a gain. The language of 'gain', therefore, does not preclude critique by Paul the Christian. Indeed, the references to 'counting / considering' in verses 7-8 indicate that Paul is speaking of his own perceptions. The bottom line is that Paul's use of the word 'gain' does not exclude criticism of his past life — whether legalistic or otherwise. In fact, it is possible that the language of 'gain' or 'profit' reflects the legalistic mind-set of building merit. If so, it fits perfectly with Paul's description of his works giving him a reason for 'confidence in the flesh'.

Finally, the fact that Paul was 'blameless' with regard to the righteousness in the law does not mean that he saw himself as attaining to righteousness.[54] Nor does it mean that he did not see inability to keep the law as the problem. Paul's statement that he was 'blameless' with regard to the righteousness in the law refers to exemplary conformity to an observable standard of conduct.[55] It certainly does not refer to sinless perfection, or the actual attainment of the true righteousness that God requires. Furthermore, Paul clearly saw himself under Judaism as a great sinner (cf., e.g., 1 Tim. 1:15). These ideas are at the heart of his belief in inability to earn one's salvation — the fact that all are sinners and so cannot perfectly keep the law of God. We return to this topic in the next chapter.

CONCLUSION

The evidence for legalism in first-century Judaism is striking and the denial of its presence is equally startling. The proponents of the NPP all define 'legalism' extremely narrowly (weighing of merits against demerits, Pelagianism). But the belief that Jews were 'saved' by God's grace plus their works, traditionally seen as legalism, is clearly present in Jewish writings. And the testimony of Jesus and Paul confirms this.

There is no question that the attempt to portray Judaism in the best possible light is a response to anti-Semitism in a post-Holocaust world. So let us say clearly that we deplore anti-Semitism in all of its manifestations. But we do not believe that the critique of someone's religious views is necessarily 'anti' anyone. We need to remember that both Jesus and Paul were Jews! They spoke critically of the legalism of their fellow Jews, but they can hardly be charged with anti-Semitism. Christian groups often fall into legalism. Are we anti-Christian because of that assertion?

Throughout this chapter we have skirted an issue that is vital to the current debate — namely, what is the nature of the law? How did Paul understand its purpose? What is the relationship between law and gospel? What is Paul's understanding of 'the works of the law'? Chapter 4 is devoted to these questions, although it can only provide a brief overview of the issues involved. Along the way, we will also show once again where we part company with the NPP.

4.

COVENANT, LAW AND 'WORKS OF THE LAW' IN PAUL'S THEOLOGY

In our age, proper reflection on the place of God's law is vital. The church is under threat from two directions. On the one side, we face the pressure, especially endemic to our age, of antinomianism (literally, being 'against law'). The law of God is being trampled in the streets. Many churches are wilting under the pressure to set aside biblical commands. On the other side, the church faces the danger of legalism — making law-observance instrumental in justification. The danger of legalism is the loss of the gospel, which is the power of God unto salvation. The NPP calls into question the traditional evangelical understanding of the law and its relationship to the gospel.

In the previous chapter, we danced around the issue of Paul's understanding of the law. The buzzword of the NPP, 'covenantal nomism', is an attempt to describe the relationship of the law to the biblical covenants. Furthermore, the problem of legalism in first-century Judaism, which we see but the NPP denies, is a misuse of the law and so raises the question of the law's proper use. These are issues that we need to explore in further depth in this chapter. Ultimately, the problems of the NPP stem not simply from an inaccurate historical understanding of first-century Judaism. They stem from an inadequate understanding of the biblical covenants.

Some of the earliest questions for Paul after his conversion must surely have revolved around the law. If salvation does not come through rigorous law-observance, as Paul seems to have thought, what was the purpose of the law? Why did God give the law? What is the relationship between the covenant God made with Israel on Mount Sinai and the new covenant? What role does the law play in the life of the Christian? These are some of the questions that we will take up in this chapter.

Paul's teaching on the law, and the question of the relationship between law and gospel, is one of the most complex and difficult issues in biblical interpretation. We certainly cannot do it justice in a single chapter. We will attempt simply to give an overview of Paul's thought on this matter, tracing certain avenues in his thinking and pointing the reader to other helpful resources. Along the way we will show where the NPP differs from the classical Reformed view and why we consider the latter to be superior.

There has been great diversity within the Reformed tradition regarding precisely how to describe the relationship between law and gospel.[1] Not all will agree with the formulations of this book. But there is in the Reformed tradition broad agreement regarding the place and purpose of the law, and that agreement is largely at odds with the positions held by those in the NPP. We will focus primarily on those areas in the NPP that are a departure from the historic Reformed consensus.

At the outset, we express our appreciation for much of what the NPP teaches with regard to Paul and the law. The treatments of both Dunn and Wright are often quite helpful and insightful. Wright's book *The Climax of the Covenant* is in many ways a masterful work filled with fresh insights that are wise and judicious. In particular, we appreciate the NPP's effort to bring out the positive nature of the law and the grace of it. In these respects, in a limited way we stand closer to some NPP advocates than we do to certain of our evangelical brothers and sisters. Unfortunately, the writings of Dunn and

Wright also contain significant errors that distort the whole. Some of these, as we shall see in chapters 5-6, seriously affect their understanding of Paul's doctrine of justification by faith. But most of the problems, as we see them, revolve around their defective understanding of first-century Judaism, and especially their failure properly to place the Mosaic covenant within the history of redemption.

We will begin by looking at Paul's use of the term 'law' and the meaning of 'law' in his writings. We will then proceed to look at the nature and purpose of the law, especially in the light of God's covenants with his people, interacting along the way with the notion of 'covenantal nomism'. With these considerations in mind, we will then move on to a critique of Dunn's understanding of the 'works of the law'.

THE MEANING OF 'LAW' IN PAUL'S WRITINGS

If we are going to understand Paul's use of the law, we need to discuss the meaning of the term 'law' in his epistles. Actually, it would be better to talk about the 'meanings' (plural), since Paul can use the term 'law' in a number of different ways. As we shall see, however, one predominant meaning does emerge, and many of the other senses in which the term is used are variations on that primary meaning.

The Greek word for 'law' is *nomos* (from which comes the term 'covenantal nomism' — see chapter 3). The word *nomos* was regularly used in the Septuagint, the Greek translation of the Old Testament, to translate the Hebrew word *Torah*. *'Torah'* can mean 'law', 'teaching', or 'instruction'. But it also came to refer to the first five books of Moses. This background is foundational for Paul, but he can use *nomos* in an even broader way.

We can understand the various uses of 'law' by Paul when we consider that in English we can use the word 'law' in different ways. We speak, for example, of the 'law of gravity'.

This 'law' is something that has been scientifically proven and is always true. We can also speak of the 'laws of the state'. These are regulations that control the life of a particular people in a specific geographic area. Though many of these laws may reflect an eternal moral law, the laws of different countries are not identical to one another. These laws, then, are not always as ironclad as the law of gravity. We can sometimes refer to 'the law' in an informal sense as a reference to the police or the authorities, those who enforce the law (e.g., 'I'm going to call the law'). 'Law' can also mean the way things generally function ('the law of supply and demand'), or it can describe a certain state of affairs ('the law of the jungle').

Similarly, Paul uses the word 'law' in a variety of ways.

Sometimes he uses 'law' to refer to *Scripture*. At times, 'law' appears to mean specifically the Pentateuch, the five books of Moses. For example, in 1 Corinthians 9:8-9, Paul asks, 'Does not the Law say the same?' and he particularly goes on to refer to and quote from 'the Law of Moses'. On one occasion (Rom. 3:21), Paul uses the phrase 'the Law and the Prophets', which seems to mean the Pentateuch and everything else in the Old Testament.

At other times, 'law' means the whole of the Old Testament. For example, in Romans 3:19 Paul refers to 'whatever the law says' after a list of Scripture quotations that includes passages from Isaiah and the Psalms. In 1 Corinthians 14:21 he introduces a quotation from Isaiah with the words, 'In the Law it is written…' This use of 'law' probably reflects the Jewish view of Paul's day that Torah was the heart of Scripture.

On other occasions, Paul seems to use 'law' in the sense of *'principle'*, though these are a matter of debate (cf. Rom. 3:27; 7:21,23,25 [the second occurrence of the word]). Some scholars think that even in these cases 'law' refers to the Mosaic law, and in particular to the way that the law is used.[2] This may be correct, although the clearest usage of law as 'principle', in our view, is in Romans 7:23, and so the term is probably used in the same sense in the other verses listed above.[3] In the light of the rest of the uses of 'law' in Romans, however, at the very least we can say that Paul is using word-play set against the predominant usage.

The principal way in which Paul uses 'law' is to refer to *the Mosaic law*, and specifically to that which was given to Moses on Mount Sinai. But even this statement needs to be carefully nuanced. Paul can sometimes use 'law' to refer to the law given on Mount Sinai in a wider sense, and sometimes he employs it to refer more narrowly to specific aspects of that law.

In the wider sense, we would define 'law' as the Mosaic covenant (or even the Mosaic order of things) at the heart of which are the commandments and stipulations of God. In Romans 5:13-14 Paul links the law to Moses, referring to the period from Adam to Moses as the time before the law was given. In Galatians 3 Paul compares the 'promise' made to Abraham with the law, which was given 430 years after the promise — that is, given to Moses on Mount Sinai (v. 17). In fact, Paul uses the language of 'covenant' in this context, referring to the 'covenant previously ratified by God' (v. 17) and later contrasting the 'two covenants' (Gal. 4:24). Thus when Paul refers to the law he has in mind the Mosaic coven-ant. This is in line with Old Testament usage, where the Mosaic law is repeatedly referred to as a 'covenant' (Deut. 17:2; 2 Kings 18:12; 2 Chr. 6:11; Jer. 11:2-4).

At the heart of this covenant are the commandments and stipulations of God. In the Old Testament, the covenant can be obeyed or transgressed (Deut. 17:2; 2 Kings 18:12). God 'commanded' his people to keep the 'words of [the] covenant' (Jer. 11:2-4). Similarly, in the New Testament, Paul consist-ently highlights the commanding aspect of the law. He speaks of doing what the law requires (Rom. 2:13-14; 10:5; Gal. 3:10), fulfilling the law (Rom. 8:4), and even breaking it (Rom. 2:23,25,27). In fact, in Paul's writings 'law' is sometimes equivalent to 'commandment(s)' (Rom. 7:7-12).

We will explain more fully below why covenant and commandments are so intricately tied together. For now, however, it is important to see that the majority of Paul's uses of 'law' focus narrowly on the divine requirements of the Mosaic covenant. Law as covenant and law as command are intricately linked to one another. Yet it is also important when reading Paul to keep these categories distinct.

Paul also uses other variations of 'law' in a narrow sense, focusing on particular aspects of the law. In 1 Corinthians 9:20-22, he speaks of his desire to save both Jews and Gentiles 'by all means' (v. 22). To those under the law, Jews, he became 'as one under the law' to win those under the law (v. 20). To those 'outside' the law (Gentiles) he became 'as one outside the law' to win those outside the law (v. 21).

But Paul makes an important contrast in verses 20-21. On the one hand, he states that he becomes 'as one' who is 'under the law' even though he himself is 'not ... under the law' (v. 20). On the other hand, he becomes 'as one' who is 'outside the law' even though he is 'not ... outside the law' (v. 21). How can Paul be both under the law and not under the law?

The easiest way to resolve this is to see that Paul is making a distinction between various aspects of the Mosaic law — namely, between the moral and ceremonial aspects. When he is among Jews, for the sake of the gospel so as not to give offence, he observes Jewish ceremonial law, even though he does not consider himself to be under those aspects of the law. On the other hand, he is not as concerned about those aspects when he is ministering to Gentiles, even though he makes clear that he is not antinomian — he is bound to God's moral law. His reference to the 'law of Christ' in verse 21 means the law as fulfilled in Christ. We see the outworking of this in Paul's ministry when, on the one hand, he has Timothy circumcised so as not to give offence to Jews (Acts 16:3), but refuses to circumcise Titus under a different set of circumstances (Gal. 2:3).

It is clear, then, that Paul can distinguish the moral from the ceremonial law. We see another example of this in Romans 2:12-16, where he contrasts those 'without the law' (Gentiles) from those 'under the law' (Jews). Yet, even though Gentiles do not have the law, 'the work of the law is written on their hearts' (2:15). The implication of this is that Paul believes in a moral law that predates the Mosaic administration — indeed, it is eternal because it is rooted in the character of God. Thus it applies to all nations, in contrast to various ceremonial laws that applied only to Israel during one period of redemptive history.

Romans 6:14 is another example of 'law' used in a narrow sense, though in a different way from what we have just seen. Paul states, 'For sin will have no dominion over you, since you are not under law but under grace.' The meaning here cannot simply be 'under the Mosaic covenant', unless we wanted to argue that all old-covenant believers were ruled by sin and did not experience grace.

It is possible that 'not under law' means not under the law's condemnation, an interpretation that makes sense in the light of Romans 8:1: 'There is … no condemnation for those who are in Christ Jesus.' It is more likely, however, that the law / grace contrast refers to their respective weakness and power. The law commands, but is powerless, because of sinful flesh, to enable human beings to fulfil its requirements (Rom. 8:3-4). 'Grace', in Paul's writings, refers not only to God's unmerited favour, but also to God's powerful work in the lives of his people (cf., e.g., Rom. 12:3,6; 15:15). Those who are 'under grace', then, are able to fulfil 'the righteous requirement of the law' (Rom. 8:4), while those who are under the law apart from grace are ruled by sin. They know the holy commandments of God, but are unable finally to carry them out. This interpretation makes sense of the larger context of Romans 6 – 8, where Paul is discussing not God's grace in justification (as in chapters 1 – 4), but his grace in sanctification and the believer's obedience to the law. It also makes sense of the fact that in this one context, being 'under the law' is practically equivalent to being 'in sin' (cf. Rom. 6:1).

To sum up, Paul's use of 'law' is diverse. It can refer to Scripture, in the sense of the Pentateuch or the whole of the Old Testament, and can also have a general meaning of 'principle'. Its predominant use is in reference to the Mosaic law. But even here 'law' can be understood in a wider sense of the Mosaic covenant, or Mosaic order of things, and in a narrower sense of the divine requirements. However, Paul also distinguishes between moral and ceremonial aspects of that law, and he even highlights the weakness of the law in distinction from God's grace.

This last point raises the question of the grace of the law. Is there grace in the law, or does Paul make an absolute distinction between law and grace, and therefore between law and gospel? We will argue that while it is possible to be under the law apart from grace (see above), the law itself is essentially gracious. We turn to that discussion now.

THE NATURE OF THE LAW

1. The grace of law

Classic Reformed theology, as contained for example in the *Westminster Confession of Faith*, has understood God's relationship to his people in terms of two covenants — the covenant of works and the covenant of grace. Let's begin first by asking, 'What is a covenant?' 'Covenant' is simply a word that describes a formal relationship between two or more parties. The Bible, for instance, talks about marriage as a covenant (cf. Mal. 2:14). A covenant is a binding relationship, a 'bond in blood', as one writer describes it.[4]

Although there are many covenants in the Bible, the basic outline of God's relationship to his people can be set forth in terms of two basic covenants. The first is the covenant of works. This was made with Adam in the Garden of Eden. It promised blessings to Adam and his family if he perfectly kept the commands of God. We call it a covenant of works because Adam's continuation in the covenant relationship depended on his perfect obedience. When Adam sinned, that particular covenant relationship was broken. God pronounced the curses of the covenant and drove the man and the woman from the garden, from his presence and from access to the tree of life (Gen. 3:14-24).

In the midst of God's pronouncement of the covenant curses, he gave the promise of an offspring of the woman who would crush the serpent's head (Gen. 3:15). This is a clear reference to Christ and a beginning to God's covenant of grace. It is a covenant of grace because it depends not on what Adam and Eve and their other descendants do. Rather, it depends on what he, the offspring, does. The rest of Scripture traces this covenant of grace.

In the Old Testament we see this covenant of grace most explicitly in the covenant that God makes with Abraham. This covenant, of course, is crucial for Paul's arguments in Galatians 3. Theologians have been in agreement that this is a gracious covenant, in which God promises to bless Abraham with countless offspring and through him to bless the nations.

A striking example of the grace of this covenant comes in Genesis 15. What appears to modern readers to be a gruesome activity is actually a vivid description of an ancient covenant-making ceremony. In this ceremony, the persons entering into a covenant with one another would take animals and literally cut them in two (because of this, the Old Testament frequently refers to the 'cutting' of a covenant). Then, those entering into the relationship would pass between the pieces as a way of saying, 'If I break this covenant, may what has happened to these animals happen to me.'

What is amazing about Genesis 15 is that *God* passes through the pieces symbolically in the smoking pot and flaming torch (Gen. 15:17). God is saying that if this covenant is broken, he will allow himself to be destroyed, not Abraham and his seed. What a beautiful example of grace! Of course, this foreshadows the Son of God, who is cut off and bears the curse of the law for his people (cf. Gal. 3:13).

After these startling promises, the book of Genesis ends and Exodus begins with God's people, the descendants of Abraham, not in the land promised to Abraham, but in slavery in Egypt. What has become of the covenant and the promises that God made with Abraham?

The book of Exodus makes clear that God's covenant with Israel on Mount Sinai through Moses is a continuation of the covenant of grace that God made with Abraham. We read, for example, in Exodus 2:24 that 'God heard [the Israelites'] groaning, and God remembered his covenant with Abraham, with Isaac, and with Jacob.' God reaches out in grace to deliver his people from slavery. Because of this, Reformed theology has historically understood the Mosaic covenant to be a manifestation, or dispensation, of the covenant of grace. This is the position, for instance, of the *Westminster Confession of Faith* (cf. 7.5).

2. Law, gospel and works

This picture, however, is complicated by the fact that the Mosaic covenant highlights law, or the 'legal' aspect — 'Do this and you will live.' This is made even more difficult by statements that Paul makes to the effect that the law teaches not faith, but works. For instance, in Galatians 3:12 he states, 'But the law is not of faith, rather, "The one who does them shall live by them"' (quoting Lev. 18:5). Paul, in other words, seems to say that the law teaches works, not grace and faith.

This raises the important, but extremely thorny, issue of the relationship between the law and the gospel, the old (Mosaic) covenant and the new covenant. Is there continuity between the two, or is there contrast? Or is there in some sense both continuity and contrast?

The legal aspect of the Mosaic covenant has led many to argue that it is a covenant of works, and therefore to emphasize discontinuity between law and gospel, between old and new covenants. This has been the position of dispensationalists. But even many Reformed theologians have argued that the Mosaic covenant is a form of the original covenant of works. In fact there was great debate among Puritan writers over this very issue leading up to the Westminster Assembly.

In a book that we highly recommend, entitled *The Grace of Law*, Ernest Kevan has shown that many of the differences between the Puritans as to whether the Mosaic law was a covenant of grace or a covenant of works were actually more apparent than real. In other words, while there were different formulations, there was widespread agreement over the following points. First, the Mosaic covenant was a part of the covenant of grace and so in its essence was gracious. Secondly, there is in the Mosaic covenant some form of reminder of the principle of the covenant of works, even if it is not itself strictly speaking a covenant of works. Thirdly, the Mosaic covenant is ultimately subservient to the new covenant in Christ Jesus. Let's look briefly at each of these three statements.

a. The Mosaic covenant was a part of the covenant of grace and so in its essence was gracious

Exodus 2:24 makes clear that the Mosaic covenant is part of God's covenant of grace. If it is part of the covenant of grace, it must in its essence be gracious. In fact, the grace of the law is evident in many ways. To begin with, the opening statement of God's giving the Ten Commandments on Mount Sinai recalls God's act of redemption for his people Israel: 'I am the LORD your God, who brought you out of the land of Egypt, out of the house of slavery' (Exod. 20:2). The giving of the law, then, is rooted in God's gracious, redemptive activity. Next, the giving of the law to Israel graciously makes known God's ways and standards to his people. The Old Testament indicates that God's giving of the law to Israel, and not to the nations, is an indication of his grace and love for Israel (Ps.

147:19-20; cf. Deut. 7:6-9), and the New Testament echoes this very idea (Rom. 3:1-2). In addition, God's provision of sacrifices to deal with sins is a further indication of the grace of the Mosaic covenant.

On this last point we should pause in anticipation of our later discussion to say that the understanding of Old Testament sacrifices is one place where we take issue with the NPP. The NPP sees sacrifices as an indication of the gracious nature of Judaism, but it fails to understand these sacrifices in the light of the new covenant. From a new-covenant perspective, it is important to understand that the blood of bulls and goats cannot take away sin. The sacrifices prescribed in the law were intended to point Israelites to Christ, the only sufficient sacrifice for sin. The grace of old-covenant sacrifices is not grace apart from this Christological focus.

b. There is in the Mosaic covenant some form of reminder, or 're-exhibition',[5] of the covenant of works, even if it is not itself strictly speaking a covenant of works

The Mosaic covenant contains the principle of the covenant of works, even though it is not a covenant of works. We cannot understand it as a covenant of works in the same sense as the covenant with Adam because the situations were different. Adam could have fulfilled his covenant. Israel after the Fall could not. So it is clear that the Mosaic law was not a covenant of works in the sense of setting forth works as the path to justification. For example, Jesus' words to the rich ruler (Matt. 19:17; Luke 18:20) should clearly not be understood as prescribing works as the way to salvation.[6]

At the same time, the law contains the principle of the covenant of works. The law, as Paul indicates, commands, 'Do this and you will live.' The law promises blessings for obedience and curses for disobedience (cf. Deut. 27 – 28). Why? There are two reasons for this. On the one hand, life at its best is life in conformity to the commands of God. As Roger Nicole has said, 'You can not break the law of God;

you can only break yourself on it.' The moral law of God is the bedrock principle of the universe. Those who live contrary to it live to their own peril.

On the other hand, the law demands obedience because the holy and righteous God demands perfect righteousness from those who are in fellowship with him. This is what we learn from the covenant of works, and in a sense that covenant has never been abrogated. The law teaches us God's standard of perfection. So Paul can write, 'For all who rely on works of the law are under a curse; for it is written, "Cursed be everyone who does not abide by all things written in the Book of the Law, and do them"' (Gal. 3:10). Similarly, James says that 'Whoever keeps the whole law but fails in one point has become accountable for all of it' (James 2:10). Perfect obedience is the standard for the one seeking to be justified by the law.

This leads us then to our third point.

c. The Mosaic covenant is ultimately subservient to the new covenant in Christ Jesus

The law, in the sense of the old covenant, is subservient to the new covenant in Christ Jesus. Paul makes a striking statement in Galatians 3:21 that highlights both the continuity and the discontinuity between the old and new covenants. He asks the question, 'Is the law then contrary to the promises of God?' He then gives the answer: 'Certainly not! For if a law had been given that could give life, then righteousness would indeed be by the law.' There is clear continuity in the covenants — the law is not contrary to the covenant of grace made with Abraham. One reason we know this is the fact that the law was not given to be a means of life in itself. Why? Because no one can fully keep it.

The law itself does not save. It is precisely this feature of the law that indicates its continuity with the covenant of grace. If someone could be saved by keeping the law, then the law would be in opposition to justification by grace through faith.

The law, then, plays an important role in the working out of God's purposes. Yet it clearly plays a subservient role in relation to the new covenant. The language that Paul uses in Galatians 3 indicates this subservient role. First, Paul clearly gives primacy to the 'promise', or the 'covenant' made with Abraham, over the law given to Moses on Mount Sinai (cf. Gal. 3:15-19). Secondly, Paul says that the law was 'added' for a specific purpose — namely, 'because of transgressions' (Gal. 3:19). Thirdly, the role of the law is ultimately that of 'guardian', or 'tutor', to lead people to Christ (Gal. 3:24).[7]

The law is therefore subservient to the coming of Christ and the new covenant. For Paul, the promise made to Abraham is given to his 'seed' — that is, Christ (Gal. 3:16). So ultimately the covenant with Abraham points to Christ. In the same way, the Mosaic covenant, which was 'added' to the one made with Abraham, also points to Christ.

In this sense, we can understand Paul's comment that Christ is the 'completion' of the law (Rom. 10:4), to use Calvin's translation.[8] Christ completes the law. The law is incomplete without him.

We will look more at the purpose of the law below, but first, with this outline of redemptive history in place, we can make some comments about the NPP and its view of the law and God's covenants.

3. The new perspective and covenant theology

A failure to understand the law within the larger perspective of God's covenants has led the proponents of the NPP into many theological and biblical errors. We can only briefly discuss some of these here.

a. The grace of the law ceases to be grace without the larger biblical picture

From a Pauline and biblical perspective, you cannot divorce the law from the one who completes the law — that is, Christ. Any attempt to do so distorts the law and inevitably leads to legalism. The attempt to keep the law, and even to find atonement in the sacrifices provided in the law, is futile, and amounts to offering one's own works to God to merit God's approval.

This is precisely the insight of the apostle Paul after his conversion on the road to Damascus. The Jews, who possessed the law and the covenants (Rom. 9:4), did not pursue righteousness in the correct way (Rom. 9:30 – 10:3) because they pursued it apart from Christ, the completion of the law (Rom. 10:4). Thus the argument of the NPP that, because Judaism was 'gracious', Paul did not have a problem with Judaism *per se* (Sanders), or that Paul's problem with Judaism was not its legalism but its exclusivism (Dunn and Wright), fails to understand the full import of Paul's theology. The grace of Judaism ceases to be grace apart from Christ.

b. The NPP flattens the covenants and fails to understand the unique role of the Mosaic covenant within the covenant of grace

There is nothing new in the NPP's conclusion that the law is gracious. As we have seen, the Reformed tradition since the Reformation has largely held to that. But the NPP fails to explain the nuances of what this grace means and what it does not mean.

The law must be seen as operating on two levels. On the one hand, the law served to order the life of God's people Israel. In this sense, it served a positive function. At this level, Israel's continuation in the land and ongoing enjoyment of covenant privileges did not depend on perfect obedience to the law. One sin did not drive them into exile. They maintained their covenant blessings until the situation became too

bad and God brought upon them the physical and material
curses of the covenant (Deut. 27 – 28). When this happened,
the elect and non-elect alike were both driven into exile. Thus
Daniel and his friends are in Babylon, but so are the idolaters
and other unbelieving Jews.

On the other hand, though Paul affirms the goodness of
the law — it is given by God, after all, and as such is holy, just
and good (Rom. 7:12) — in various places he highlights its
peculiar negative function. The law serves a 'ministry of
condemnation' (2 Cor. 3:4-11). It causes people to recognize
their sin, and so it drives them to Christ (Gal. 3:24). The law
in this latter sense, then, serves God's greater purposes of
grace, but it does so in a negative way.

Robert L. Dabney has said, 'In truth, the transaction of
God with Israel was twofold: it had its shell and its kernel; its
body and its spirit; its type, and its antitype. The corporate,
theocratic, political nation was the shell; the elect seed were
the kernel.'[9]

The NPP merges these aspects. They treat the 'social,
political' aspects and the 'spiritual' aspects, the type and the
antitype, at the same level. So they merge being saved with
being part of the covenant community. This is a grave error
that has serious consequences for understanding salvation in
biblical perspective. It is no wonder, then, as we shall see in
chapters 5-6, that the NPP largely treats justification as a
social construct.

At the same time, the NPP flattens the covenants by
failing to see the unique and subservient role of the Mosaic
covenant within the covenant of grace. As Paul says, the law
was 'added' to the promise (Gal. 3:19). Understanding the law
as gracious, apart from its negative role of driving people to
Christ, distorts the grace of the law.

c. The NPP treats Paul's theology, like that of Judaism, as conforming to the pattern of 'covenantal nomism'

In other words, according to the new perspective, Paul in essence teaches that one enters the covenant by grace and remains in the covenant by works. But this is a clear distortion that becomes evident when we look at the nature of the covenants.

In the covenant of works, the key issue is *what human beings do*. This is clear in the case of Adam. But we also see a reminder in the Mosaic covenant, which teaches that 'the one who does these things will live by them'. In the covenant of grace, the heart of the covenant is *what God and Christ will do*. This is what makes the covenant of grace gracious. Of course, God's people are to respond to God's grace in thankful obedience to his law. Indeed, those empowered by the Spirit are able to keep 'the righteous requirement of the law' (Rom. 8:4). The New Testament opposes antinomianism (Rom. 3:31; 6:1-14; cf. John 14:15). But the works of God's people do not keep them in the covenant. In fact, covenantal nomism is exactly what Paul is combating in Galatians and elsewhere.[10]

To put it differently, there is no such thing as an unconditional covenant. All covenants carry demands and stipulations. The crucial issue is, in whose works are we resting? The covenant of grace says:

> Thy works, not mine, O Christ, speak gladness to this
>   heart;
> They tell me all is done, they bid my fear depart.
>
> Thy righteousness, O Christ, alone can cover me;
> No righteousness avails save that which is of thee.[11]

The bottom line is that we *are* saved by works — not those of human beings, which are like filthy rags, but those of Jesus Christ. His perfect righteousness fulfils the demands of God and that righteousness is graciously given to those who trust in him.

The NPP's failure to comprehend the larger biblical picture of the covenants goes hand in hand with their denial of the doctrine of the imputation of Christ's righteousness. We will return to that issue in chapter 6. For our purposes in this chapter, we need to look further at the NPP's denial of one other traditional evangelical doctrine — namely, that the law was intended to drive people to Christ (the so-called 'second use' of the law). We turn, then, to lay out more fully, albeit in abbreviated fashion, Paul's understanding of the purpose of the law.

THE PURPOSE OF THE LAW

As we have seen earlier, Reformed Christians have traditionally understood there to be three uses of the law. First, the law reveals God's standards of righteousness, and in so doing it guides God's people and restrains evil. In this sense, the law was a gracious gift to Israel, as it directed corporate and individual life. Secondly, the law convicts sinners and drives them to Christ. Thirdly, the law is a guide to Christians in their daily life of obedience to God.

We need to recognize that Paul was not composing systematic theology texts. He was writing occasional letters, sent to particular churches for specific purposes. We should not expect, therefore, that at any one point Paul is going to lay out fully his view regarding the purpose or purposes of the law. But we find plenty of teaching in his letters, which, when combined, confirms the three uses of the law listed above.

New perspective adherents primarily deny the second use of the law. We will focus our discussion there. We can summarize Paul's teaching with regard to the law's 'negative' function as follows: the law exposes sin; the law provokes sin; and the law condemns sin.[12]

1. The law was 'added because of transgressions'

We have already looked briefly at Paul's teaching on the law in Galatians 3. There we see a clear statement of his under-standing of the purpose of the law. After contrasting the law and the promise and making clear that justification is not by the law, Paul raises the logical question: 'Why then the law?' (v. 19). His answer initially seems ambiguous: 'It was added because of transgressions.' This statement has been the subject of much debate.

James Dunn, in an attempt to get around a negative purpose of the law, interprets this statement positively: the law provided an interim measure of offering sacrifice for sin until the problem of transgression could be definitively and finally dealt with on the cross.[13] According to Dunn, God would be 'remarkably heartless' if he failed to provide this remedy. This interpretation is implausible at best. First, it introduces a foreign notion into the text at this point, that God positively provided a remedy for Israel's sin in the law. Secondly, it does not take into account the statements that Paul makes in verses 21 and 22, where it is apparent that he is focusing on the negative aspects of the law. In verse 21 Paul is forced to ask, 'Is the law … contrary to the promises of God?' He would not ask that question if he had not intro-duced a concept that seems to contradict God's larger pur-poses for his people. In verse 22 Paul's meaning becomes clear: Scripture imprisoned everything under sin, so that the promise by faith in Jesus Christ might be given to those who believe. 'Because of transgressions' is closely linked to impris-oning all under sin, not liberating people from it through atoning sacrifice.

2. Through the law comes knowledge of sin

This interpretation is confirmed by Paul's similar statements elsewhere. In Romans 3:20 he states, 'For by works of the law no human being will be justified in his sight, since through the law comes knowledge of sin.' The law reveals sin, and thus also shows that no one can be justified through the law. No one can keep its perfect demands. The law shows all to be sinners.

This idea is repeated in Romans 7:7: 'What then shall we say? That the law is sin? By no means! Yet if it had not been for the law, I would not have known sin. I would not have known what it is to covet if the law had not said, "You shall not covet."' It is appropriate that Paul makes this statement with regard to covetousness, a sin of the heart that is easy to overlook and excuse. But the law reveals to us that covetousness is sin.

3. The law provokes sin

In addition to revealing sin, the law actually provokes sin. Paul makes this point in at least two places. In Romans 7:8 he says, 'But sin, seizing an opportunity through the commandment, produced in me all kinds of covetousness. Apart from the law, sin lies dead.' The law stimulates sin and gives rise to sin in sinful human beings. The problem is not the law, which is 'holy and righteous and good' (Rom. 7:12). The problem is the sinfulness of human beings.

Sinful human beings, rebellious in our nature, desire to transgress a commandment when we come upon it. The sign says, 'Wet paint — do not touch,' and there is a desire in us to reach out our hand and touch (the reason why we may not do so perhaps has more to do with the consequences than the desires of our heart — we don't want wet paint on our fingers!). As John Murray says, 'The more law is brought to bear upon the heart of sinful man the more the enmity of the heart is aroused to transgression.'[14]

In 1 Corinthians 15:56 Paul makes the statement: 'The sting of death is sin, and the power of sin is the law.' The law, in some sense, gives sin its power, provoking sinful human beings to pass beyond its boundaries. This passage is especially telling because in the context Paul is dealing with the resurrection, not with the law at all. This statement about sin and the law is almost an afterthought. But it reveals how closely sin and law are linked in Paul's thinking.

4. The law's purpose: to increase the trespass

In Romans 5:20 Paul states, 'Now the law came in to increase the trespass.' As in Galatians 3:19, Paul is here discussing the purpose of the law. We need to look at this verse separately from the verses above because of the debate surrounding it even among those who hold to a traditional, evangelical understanding of the law. Some argue that Paul is saying here that the purpose of the law was to increase the trespass in the sense of revealing sin and trespass.[15] Others argue that Paul is asserting that the law provokes sin and causes trespasses to be multiplied.[16] As we have seen above, both of these interpretations are fully in line with what Paul teaches elsewhere — indeed, both are even present in the larger context of his letter to the Romans.

A better interpretation, however, takes into account that Paul here uses the singular, 'trespass', as opposed to the plural. This follows on from the repeated use of the singular, 'trespass', in the immediately preceding verses, Romans 5:15-18, with regard to the sin of Adam. Paul's point, then, is that the law did not provide the solution to the problem of Adam's sin. It only served to exacerbate the problem. The result is that the reign of sin (Rom. 5:21) increased.[17]

The law, then, reveals sin and provokes sin. It exacerbates the problem of sin. To put it differently, the law intensified the problem of sin, which was already present in the world before the law was given (Rom. 5:13). Why? Because the seriousness of sin is magnified when people transgress a revealed law of God. It is with this background that we understand clearly Paul's statements about the law's 'ministry of condemnation'.

5. The law condemns sin

In 2 Corinthians 3, Paul makes clear two things about the law. The first is that the ministry of the law under Moses was glorious. The law came from God and was his holy, revealed will. But, secondly, the law brings condemnation. The ministry of the 'old covenant' (v. 14) is one of death (vv. 6-7). That of the new covenant is life (v. 6). The reason seems clear: the law pronounces curses on those who do not fully keep its requirements (Gal. 3:10; cf. Deut. 27 – 28).

The grace of the law is not in its ability to give life or bring forgiveness of sins. It is in pointing sinners to a Saviour.

6. The law in the life of Christians

Paul makes clear that, although Christians are not under the law as a 'covenant of works', in the sense of being able to be justified or condemned by it (see *Westminster Confession of Faith,* 19.6), the law continues to guide the moral life of God's people. We have already seen one example of this in 1 Corinthians 9:19-21, where Paul states, with regard to the moral law, that he is not outside the law of God. But perhaps a clearer example occurs in Romans 13:8-10. Paul commands the Roman believers to love one another (v. 8), but he goes on to quote specific commandments to show what this love looks like. He has said earlier that love must be 'genuine' (Rom. 12:9). He is aware that love can be false love, or that it can be reduced to mere sentimentality. We need specific commandments to instruct us what love looks like.[18] The Decalogue (or Ten Commandments) instructs believers in how to love God and others.

We have seen that Paul's writings uphold the three uses of the law as taught in the Reformed tradition. In particular, we have focused on the second use of the law to combat its denial among proponents of the new perspective. One key issue remains: James Dunn's interpretation of the 'works of the law'.

THE 'WORKS OF THE LAW'

James Dunn's interpretation of the phrase 'works of the law', which is largely followed by N. T. Wright, has been the subject of great debate. We need to touch briefly on this matter here.

The phrase 'works of the law' occurs eight times in Paul's letters, six times in Galatians and twice in Romans.[19] In each case, Paul denies that 'works of the law' can save or justify, and he typically contrasts 'works of the law' with faith. The traditional Reformed and evangelical interpretation has been that no one can be justified by works of the law because no one can fully keep the commands of the law. Sin causes us to fall short of God's standard. The new perspective, and especially Dunn, challenges this interpretation.

Dunn recognizes the importance of the phrase 'works of the law' in Paul's letters. He states in his commentary on Romans that 'works of the law' is 'a key phrase whose importance for understanding Paul's thought in this letter can hardly be overestimated'.[20]

Dunn, however, denies that Paul understood the phrase 'as works which earn God's favour, as merit-amassing observances'. He continues:

> They are rather seen as badges: they are simply what membership of the covenant people involves, what mark out the Jews as God's people... In other words, Paul has in view precisely what Sanders calls 'covenantal nomism'. And what he denies is ... that God's grace extends only to those who wear the badge of the covenant...[21]

The bottom line for Dunn is that when Paul opposes 'works of the law', a phrase that he consistently uses with a negative connotation (cf. the positive use of 'work of the law' in Rom. 2:15), he is opposing Jewish exclusivism, not legalism.

There is a two-pronged thrust in Dunn's interpretation of
the Pauline phrase 'works of the law' (though he points out
that it is not exclusively Pauline; it is also found in, for example, the writings of the Jewish sect at Qumran). The first is
'works of the law' as related to covenantal nomism, referring
to those works which maintain one's status within the covenant. In this sense, 'works of the law' refers to all that the law
required. Dunn asserts that 'in principle' this is what 'works of
the law' means — namely, the requirements of the law.[22]

The second key idea, the most prominent in Dunn's
writings, is that 'works of the law' take on a particular meaning as those works which most clearly distinguish Jews from
Gentiles. In other words, when the circumstances dictate, the
term 'works of the law' refers specifically to laws such as
circumcision and food laws which particularly mark Jews off
from Gentiles. It is in this sense that Dunn refers to 'works of
the law' as 'boundary-marking' ordinances. In his view, one
purpose of the law was to protect Israel from the Gentiles.
The law as a whole, then, set boundaries between Israel and
the nations. But certain laws mark this division more clearly
than others. These particular boundary markers are the focus
of Paul's polemic against 'works of the law' in his letters.

Dunn makes this point most strongly, and most persua-
sively, in dealing with Galatians. In that epistle, Paul is battling
against Jewish Christians who were forcing Gentiles to be
circumcised (Gal. 5:2-3; 6:12-13) and to keep food laws (Gal.
2:11-14) in order to be justified (Gal. 5:4; cf. Acts 15:1) and
fully accepted within the church. In this context, according to
Dunn, Paul's problem with 'works of the law' is that they
exclude Gentiles. Paul's opponents failed to understand that
the law was an interim measure (Gal. 3:19-25). With the
coming of Christ, the 'works of the law' should no longer
divide believers in Jesus Christ. The barriers have been
broken down. The key issue, then, is unity, whereas strict
adherence to 'works of the law' brings division.

We agree with Dunn that unity is one major problem that Paul is addressing in Galatians. Indeed, he wants Gentiles to be accepted as full believers without the necessity of their becoming Jews. He affirms that 'in Christ Jesus' all are one (Gal. 3:28). But Paul never argues that the problem with 'works of the law' is the exclusion of Gentiles, even though in one sense they do exclude Gentiles.

Rather, Paul's problem with an emphasis on 'works of the law' is twofold. First, it is a distortion of the gospel (cf. Gal. 2:5,14), the gospel that first declares forgiveness of sin in Christ Jesus and then unites all who truly trust Christ to save them. (See our discussion of Paul's gospel in chapter 2.) Secondly, Paul argues that no one can be saved by 'works of the law' because no one can fully keep the law. He states in Galatians 3:10, 'For all who rely on works of the law are under a curse; for it is written, "Cursed be everyone who does not abide by all things written in the Book of the Law, and do them."' At the same time, Paul is clear that those who rely on works of the law must do them all: 'I testify again to every man who accepts circumcision that he is bound [NASB, 'under obligation'] to keep the whole law' (Gal. 5:3).

This is the traditional reading of Paul's argument in Galatians, and it still seems to us to be the best and most natural interpretation. Dunn's argument, that the Jews have not done 'all things written in the Book of the Law' (Gal. 3:10) by their failure to recognize God's blessings going to the nations, is not convincing.[23] It ignores the important connection between Galatians 3:10 and 5:3 which highlights the importance of perfect obedience to the law.

The key issue, then, is not amassing merit in the sense of piling up more good works than bad works. We agree with Dunn in this respect. But this does not mean Paul is not opposing legalism. Dunn argues that 'works of the law' amount to covenantal nomism. But we have already argued that covenantal nomism is legalism. Essentially, Paul views the acceptance of circumcision for justification as relying on the law to save you (Gal. 5:4). But to add to faith reliance on any human work is legalism. If you are going to do this, Paul says, then you need to keep the whole of the law.

Dunn argues that Paul did not understand perfect obedience to the law to be the requirement of the law because Jews in Paul's day did not see things this way.[24] But did Paul's conversion have no effect on his theology? Through the revelation of Jesus Christ, Paul came to see that even a 'blameless' life in Judaism (Phil. 3:6) does not produce the righteousness that God requires.

Ultimately for Paul the problem with law-observance as a way of salvation is human sin. This is what he spells out so powerfully in his letter to the Romans. In Romans 3:20 he states, 'For by works of the law no human being will be justified in his sight, since through the law comes knowledge of sin.' The picture is then complete. The problem with 'works of the law' is not the demand of God, which is holy and good. The problem is that, because of sin, no fallen human being can meet God's demand for righteousness. Outside of Christ, who is the completion of the law and the one sufficient atonement for sin, all human striving is legalism.

Dunn's exposition of Romans in this respect once again is wanting. He claims that Paul is primarily combating Jewish privilege and distinction (cf. Rom. 2:1-4,17-24; 3:27-31). A critique of Jewish superiority is indeed present in these chapters. Paul is intending to show Jews that they too have sinned — 'all have sinned and fall short of the glory of God' (Rom. 3:23) — and so they, like Gentiles, are under God's wrath and condemnation. Works of the law do not save because, like Abraham, no one has a boast before God (Rom. 4:2), all are 'ungodly' (Rom. 4:5), and the blessing of righteousness ultimately rests on the one whose sins are forgiven (4:6-8). When Paul, from the law, spells out Israel's transgression of the law (Rom. 3:10-18), not once does he list Israel's exclusion of Gentiles as the reason they fail to attain God's righteousness.

Let us boil the argument down in this way: our fundamental disagreement with Dunn is his denial that for Paul perfect obedience to the law is necessary for salvation, because, Dunn argues, it is contrary to Jewish belief in Paul's day and because God has provided sacrifices to deal with sin. We agree that Paul, and probably a large portion of Judaism in Paul's day, did not believe perfect obedience to the law was possible. Most Jews were not relying on their perfect obedience to save them.

But Dunn's assertion misses the point. Paul is arguing that if you seek justification in the law, adding works of the law to faith, then you must observe the whole law. It does not matter whether Paul and other Jews were actually pursuing perfect obedience to the law or not. Paul came to see that God's standard is perfection (cf. Matt. 5:48). He now understood that the pursuit of righteousness apart from Christ, who is the completion of the law, is legalism. Whether it be circumcision or baptism or anything else, human works contribute nothing to our salvation.

The reliance on circumcision amounts to reliance on the law, and the one who relies on the law must keep all of it. The one who lives by the law dies by the law because the law pronounces a curse on disobedience. Thus Paul says it is faith — faith alone! — in Christ alone that saves. Faith plus circumcision — or any other work — is a false gospel, not primarily because it excludes Gentiles (though it may also do that), but because it subjects people to God's curse. No one can offer to God the righteousness that he requires.

Dunn (as well as Wright) seems to have the impression that if he can show from the context that Paul is dealing with the issue of the unity of Jewish and Gentile believers, then Paul must primarily be opposing the exclusion of the Gentiles. But once again the NPP forces on us here a false dichotomy. Paul's arguments primarily deal with the nature of justification — it comes through faith, not works of the law. And because justification is through faith, human distinctions are levelled, human boasting is obliterated, and God's faithful people can live together humbly in love and unity.

This picture is confirmed by looking at other places in Paul's letters where Paul does not use the full phrase 'works of the law', but affirms simply that we are saved by faith and not by 'works'. The most striking example of this comes in Ephesians 2:8-9 (cf. also Titus 3:5; 2 Tim. 1:9). Paul is primarily addressing Gentile converts in this passage, using the second person, telling them that 'you were dead in ... trespasses and sins' (Eph. 2:1). In verse 3 he switches to the first person plural, affirming that 'we ... were by nature children of wrath, like the rest of mankind'. But he returns to the second person in the climactic statement in 2:8-9: 'For by grace you have been saved through faith. And this is not your own doing; it is the gift of God, not a result of works, so that no one may boast.'

Paul is clearly not speaking here of Jewish works done in obedience to the law, nor of Jewish boasting of their privileged status over Gentiles. He is plainly speaking of human ability to boast in achieving one's own salvation. But no one can accomplish this, because all are under sin — by nature, we are those who deserve God's wrath. Thus salvation is only by God's grace, through our faith — and even this is a gift of God. It is because God has brought salvation in this way that the dividing wall of hostility has been broken down and Jews and Gentiles can be united in the body of Christ (Eph. 2:11-22).

Dunn does not believe that Paul wrote Ephesians, Colossians and the Pastoral Epistles.[25] This is why passages like Ephesians 2 carry so little weight for him. But for those who affirm Pauline authorship of all the letters that bear his name, passages like Ephesians 2 confirm the correctness of the traditional evangelical and Reformed interpretation of Paul.

CONCLUSION

This chapter has attempted to respond to the NPP in the area where it is probably the strongest — namely, in its presentation of the law and the biblical covenants. This aspect of the NPP, in fact, has attracted many within the Reformed camp. We share appreciation for the NPP in its emphasis on the gracious nature of the Mosaic law and in its emphasis on the centrality of the covenants in biblical theology (see especially Wright's *Climax of the Covenant*). Still, in the final analysis, the NPP's depiction of the law and the covenants is found wanting.

In this chapter, we have tried to lay out a proper view of the biblical covenants and the place of the law within them. We have seen the gracious nature of the law and yet ultimately the subservient function of the Mosaic covenant to the new covenant in Christ Jesus. We have also seen that the law contains a reminder of the original covenant of works made with Adam — 'Do this and you will live.' The law does not bring life because no one can fully keep the law. The law reveals sin, provokes sin and condemns sin.

The NPP ultimately distorts the nature of the biblical covenants. It flattens the covenants and fails to see the unique place of the law within redemptive history. The law drives men and women to Christ by causing them to recognize their sin. The law's condemnation of sinners adds a sense of urgency to this. The NPP denies this function of the law.

The NPP also distorts the grace of the law by failing to see that the law cannot be fully understood apart from Christ, the completion of the law. The gracious aspects of the law, including the sacrifices, point to Christ. Ultimately, the NPP fails to discern properly the distinction between the covenant of works and the covenant of grace. All covenants are conditional in the sense of demanding works. But what makes the covenant of grace gracious is that its demands are met by

Christ, the 'seed' of Abraham, and the benefits of Christ's obedience accrue to all who trust in him.

This conditional aspect of the covenants also sheds light on the Pauline phrase 'works of the law', those demands of the law which can never be met by sinful human beings. Paul's opposition to 'works of the law' is not to 'boundary markers', as Dunn suggests. It is, rather, to any human attempt to add a human work, such as circumcision, to faith. Reliance on the grace of God, the only path to salvation, means resting in the finished work of Christ.

We are in a position now to turn to the teaching of the NPP on justification, represented primarily in the writings of N. T. Wright. Wright's understanding of justification is marked in particular by its definition of justification in socio-logical, not soteriological terms, as well as by its denial of the doctrine of the imputation of Christ's righteousness. Both of these are rooted in an improper reckoning of the biblical covenants — especially in the flattening of the covenants and the failure to see the demand of the covenant of works. We turn to that discussion more fully now.

5.

JUSTIFICATION BY FAITH AND N. T. WRIGHT'S NARRATIVE READING OF THE BIBLE

According to Martin Luther, justification by faith is the 'doctrine on which the church stands or falls'. In the attempt to release Paul's letters from their 'Lutheran captivity', the NPP has not only moved justification out of the centre of Paul's theology, it has also redefined it. In evangelical and Reformed circles, the most significant NPP scholar to move and redefine justification is N. T. Wright. We say 'most significant' because Wright professes to be an evangelical Christian and to stand within the Reformed tradition. He is a first-class scholar and a gifted writer and speaker. His influence among evangelical scholars, especially the younger generation, has been far-reaching.

In many ways, evangelical Christians owe Wright a debt of gratitude. He has stood firm against the 'Jesus Seminar' and for the historicity of the Gospels and the literal, bodily resurrection of Christ. He has stood for biblical standards of morality within the liberal Church of England. And he believes that the Bible is our sole authority in faith and practice.

But, unfortunately, we believe Wright to be on the wrong side of one of the most critical doctrines of the church, namely, justification by faith. His teachings have caused much confusion with regard to a biblical doctrine that demands clarity. The salvation of souls depends on such clarity — as does the future of the church. We believe Wright is wrong both exegetically, in his exposition of key passages, and theologically, in his understanding of the biblical doctrine. These errors ultimately stem, at least in his presentation of them, from a faulty narrative structure imposed on the New Testament.

As we have already pointed out, Wright's brand of the NPP is very different from that of the other leading proponents. But in several key areas that affect his understanding of justification, his views are similar to those of the others. He believes Sanders' view of first-century Judaism to be 'established'.[1] With Dunn, he holds that 'works of the law' refer to Jewish boundary markers and that Paul's problem with such 'works' is that they exclude Gentiles. Like Stendahl, Wright views Paul as driven by his call to be the apostle to the Gentiles and by his determination that Gentiles, as Gentiles, should be fully accepted in a family of faith whose roots are Jewish. According to Wright, after his conversion Paul's 'prime concern ... was the admission of Gentiles into the one covenant people of Israel's god'.[2] Thus, with the rest of the NPP, Wright sees the Jew/Gentile question as pre-eminent in Paul's letters.

What sets Wright apart from the other leading proponents of the NPP is the compelling way in which he locates Paul within the larger biblical and Jewish 'story'. We will begin with a quick overview of Wright's approach and where that leads him with respect to justification. Then we will return to look at aspects of it in more detail and to offer our critique.

WRIGHT'S VIEW OF THE BIBLICAL 'STORY'

According to Wright, the basic overall story of the Bible runs as follows. The one, true, all-wise, all-powerful God created a good and perfect universe. Adam's disobedience brought sin, death, evil and misery into that creation. God chose Israel to be the 'true humanity' and God's agent to restore creation and to undo the effects of the Fall. Since the Fall, then, God's purpose has been to re-establish his wise rule — his kingdom — over all the earth.

This can be seen clearly, according to Wright, in the covenant that God made with Abraham. God's call of Abraham in Genesis 12 was a response to Adam's sin and the corrupt, fragmented life depicted in Genesis 4 – 11. God promised Abraham not only that he would bless him and his descendants, but also that he would make him the father of many nations and that all nations would be blessed in him. In other words, Wright argues, God's purpose in the covenant was to deal with the problem of sin in the world and to set the world to rights, making a single worldwide family.

The problem, however, is that the physician, Israel, became sick. God's chosen instrument to deal with sin and idolatry in the world herself fell into sin and idolatry. Thus she was unable to carry out her God-given task of being a light to the nations and bringing restoration to the world. As a result of her sin, God sent her into exile — which, in Wright's opinion, is where she remained until the coming of Christ.

This brings us then to the first-century Jewish understanding of Israel's position and role within God's larger plan for the world. This first-century Jewish 'worldview', Wright argues, is foundational for understanding the New Testament. This world-view is expressed primarily in Israel's stories, which are a reminder of her place within the single larger story. Specifically, Israel is in a state of sin and slavery, ruled by pagans. She is in the land, but still in exile. In this condition, she is unable to carry out her God-ordained mission. For God to bring his purposes to fruition, he must first rescue Israel. This is precisely what Israel longs for. Her hope is that God will indeed intervene, bringing forgiveness and redemption (a second exodus), setting the world to rights and re-establishing his kingdom over all creation.

It is within this first-century Jewish context, Wright asserts, that we must understand the nature of salvation and justification. Salvation is not a pietistic, individualistic, ahistorical rescue *from* the world. It is, rather, God's rescue of his people within history and *for* the world. As Wright puts it, the fundamental Jewish hope was for liberation from oppression, for the restoration of the land and for proper rebuilding of the temple. This in turn would lead to the restoration of all creation.[3]

Likewise, 'justification' is the 'vindication' of God's people (or at least the true remnant within Israel) over against her enemies.[4] This vindication, furthermore, is the result of their faithfulness to the covenant. Thus God also vindicates 'faithful Jews' (true Israel), setting them apart from unfaithful Jews who fail to keep Torah and give in to pagan influences. Justification — vindication — is future, coming at the time of consummation. Yet, for those who are faithful to the covenant — demonstrated by their adhering to the signs and symbols (or badges) that mark out the true covenant members — there is assurance that the true God will be faithful to them. Thus, in first-century Judaism, justification was not about how you become right with God, but how you can know who is part of the true covenant people of the one living God.[5]

This first-century Jewish world-view, Wright argues, is the defining historical context for the rise of Christianity and the New Testament. In his words, 'Paul's story is essentially the Jewish story, albeit … straightened out.'[6] According to Wright, the narrative structure remains the same, even as Jewish hopes are redefined in Jesus and beliefs are redefined in the writings of Paul.[7] The key event that effected this redefinition was the coming into the world of Jesus the Messiah, the true and representative Israelite, the fulfilment of all Israel's hopes.

Jesus came to do what Israel failed to do. He was the 'seed' of Abraham to whom the promises were made. In his death, he triumphed over Israel's enemies. His resurrection marked the ushering in of the age to come, and the hope of the 'new creation'. With the coming of Messiah Jesus, Paul understood that God was at work fulfilling his covenant promises — setting the world to rights, dealing with sin and evil, setting his people free, bringing justice on the enemies of God and calling to himself a worldwide family. This is at the heart of Paul's call to be the 'apostle to the Gentiles'.

In Messiah Jesus, Paul recognized that God was being faithful to his covenant promises for Israel and for the world. Jesus was the new Moses who released his people from slavery. By implication, then, the time had also come for the true people of God to be 'a light to the nations' and for both Jews and Gentiles to be gathered together into the single family of God. In Jesus and through the proclamation of the gospel, God is establishing his reign — his kingdom — over all creation.

For Paul the Christian, as for Paul the Jew, salvation is not an individualistic, pietistic, ahistorical rescue from the world. Similarly, Paul's proclamation of the gospel does not aim merely to transport individual souls to a disembodied state of eternal bliss. Instead, the proclamation of the gospel is the declaration that Jesus is Lord over all creation and that God is working to restore what was lost in Adam's sin. Jesus' work of salvation means that creation is being renewed and Gentiles are being blessed and brought into the people of God.

The cosmic implications and the inclusion of the Gentiles, Wright asserts, are as essential to God's work as the salvation of individuals. According to Wright, though often overlooked by traditional interpreters, the creation of a single, worldwide family is part of the core of Paul's mission and theology. Thus Paul's perspective is both covenantal and eschatological, since the coming of Messiah in fulfilment of God's covenant

promises to Abraham means that 'the end of the ages' has
come upon us.

WRIGHT'S UNDERSTANDING OF JUSTIFICATION

Briefly turning our attention to Romans, the key letter where
Paul expounds the doctrine of justification, we can see how
Wright's overall scheme affects his exegetical approach. In his
view, both covenantal and eschatological aspects of Paul's
thought are present in his statement that 'in [the gospel] the
righteousness of God is revealed' (Rom. 1:17). 'The gospel' is
the proclamation that 'Jesus is Lord', the true King and ruler
of the universe. 'The righteousness of God' is God's own
righteousness (not a righteousness that he gives to people)
and refers to his faithfulness to his covenant promises (which,
Wright claims, is simply the way Jews in the first century
would have understood it). The verb 'revealed' is *apokalupto*,
from which we get the word 'apocalyptic', a coded way of
saying that God is acting to vindicate his people and to set up
his eternal, just reign.

According to Wright, Romans 1:17 is the thematic verse of
Romans. God's righteousness — his covenant faithfulness —
is the principal theme of the letter. Justification is not the
central idea of Romans, but is linguistically tied to the word
'righteousness'. Wright defines justification both in covenantal (declaring that one is a member of the covenant) and
judicial (declaring that one is 'in the right') terms. It is God's
declaration made regarding individuals when they believe in
Messiah Jesus, but it is about more than just individuals. It
affirms that all, both Jews and Gentiles, who believe in Christ
are members of God's, and therefore Abraham's, family.

Wright argues (in many ways echoing Stendahl) that in both
Romans and Galatians, the two letters of Paul which expound
the doctrine of justification by faith, the overriding concern is
the coming together of Jewish and Gentile believers into the

single family of God. There is still room for the justification of individual sinners (properly understood). But this must be seen in the light of the larger picture. Thus Wright calls justification 'the great ecumenical doctrine'.

This overall picture is what lies behind many of the provocative statements that Wright makes which cause evangelical Christians to be uncomfortable (if not outraged). For instance, he declares, 'The doctrine of justification by faith is not what Paul means by "the gospel".'[8] When seen against the background of Wright's larger framework, this statement makes sense within his scheme. The 'gospel', as he understands it, is the declaration that 'Jesus is Lord' (Rom. 10:9) — that is, ruler of all creation (a politically dangerous statement when written to Roman Christians living where 'Caesar is Lord' was the common refrain). Justification is God's vindication of those who accept Christ's lordship.

Or again he writes, '... the gospel is not, for Paul, a message about "how one gets saved", in an individual and ahistorical sense. It is a fourfold announcement about Jesus...'[9] One can actually understand why Wright would make such a statement in an individualistic age in which much of popular evangelicalism believes that Christianity is primarily about 'Jesus and me'. (We just as quickly add, however, that the best of Reformed thought has not had such a truncated view of the Christian life, even as it affirms the essential nature of individual salvation.) According to Wright, Paul's narrative framework is essentially a reworking of Jewish beliefs and hopes for redemption and vindication within history and for the world. Thus the gospel, the announcement that God has acted in Jesus the Messiah, has important covenantal and cosmic implications.

Similarly, Wright states:

> Paul invokes the great stories of God, Israel and the world because his view of salvation itself, and with it justification and all the rest, is not an ahistorical scheme

about how individuals come into a right relationship with God, but rather tells how the God of Abraham has fulfilled his promises at last through the apocalyptic death and resurrection of his own beloved Son.[10]

According to Wright, in Christ, God has revealed his covenant faithfulness by acting to bring redemption to the world and blessing to the nations, thus establishing his kingdom over all creation. As Wright puts it, Paul conceives of 'salvation not as an *a*historical rescue *from* the world but as the *trans*historical redemption *of* the world', reflecting the Jewish narrative of Paul's upbringing.[11]

Again he says:

> 'Justification' in the first century was not about how someone might establish a relationship with God. It was about God's eschatological definition, both future and present, of who was, in fact, a member of his people. In Sanders' terms, it was not so much about 'getting in', or indeed about 'staying in', as about 'how you could tell who was in'. In standard Christian theological language, it wasn't so much about soteriology as about ecclesiology; not so much about salvation as about the church.[12]

This description of justification is in line with what we saw earlier and the view that justification is essentially God's vindication of faithful ('true') Israel over against her pagan enemies and unfaithful Jews who fail to keep the covenant. Membership in the right group, as demonstrated by adherence to the 'badges' of covenant faithfulness, was the key. Justification, for Wright, is God's declaration that those who have the right badges are 'in the right'. Thus it was about 'how you could tell who was in'.

In view of the above, Wright argues that justification by faith is primarily a doctrine that Paul taught for assurance:

... the doctrine of 'justification by faith' becomes crucially relevant in Paul's mission to the pagan world. It was not the message he would announce on the street to the puzzled pagans of (say) Corinth; it was not the main thrust of his evangelistic message. It was the thing his converts most needed to know in order to be assured that they really were part of God's people.[13]

This fits with Wright's picture of first-century Judaism in which members of the right group, who manifested the badges of covenant faithfulness, could know in the present that they would be vindicated in the future when God established his universal kingdom.

This last assertion of Wright leads to two others.

First, he claims that 'Justification by faith is a second-order doctrine.'[14] This is, of course, extremely provocative to Christians who hold with Luther that justification is 'the doctrine on which the church stands or falls'. But for Wright it follows on from the previous point. If justification by faith is not at the heart of Paul's gospel message, but taught by him to give assurance to Gentile Christians that they are part of God's family, then it is a 'second-order doctrine'.

Secondly, Wright asserts, 'We're not justified by faith by believing in justification by faith.' In many ways, this is patently true. We are justified by believing in Jesus. But we will argue in the following pages that the complex of ideas related to the traditional understanding of justification by faith must be taught for individual sinners to be justified.

Finally, Wright states:

Briefly and baldly put, if you start with the popular view of justification, you may actually lose sight of the heart of the Pauline gospel; whereas if you start with the Pauline gospel itself you will get justification in all its glory thrown in as well.[15]

In other words, if you start with justification by faith as teaching only a doctrine of the salvation of individuals, you may lose sight of the larger Pauline picture of Jesus as Lord of all creation. But when you begin with the larger picture, you also leave room for the justification of individual sinners who put their faith in Christ.

One of the practical implications of this for Wright is that justification, the doctrine that unites all who 'believe in Jesus', has been turned into its opposite — namely, a doctrine that divides. He applies this especially to the Protestant/Roman Catholic split. He states:

> Many Christians, both in the Reformation and in the counter-Reformation traditions, have done themselves and the church a great disservice by treating the doctrine of 'justification' as central to their debates, and by supposing that it described the system by which people attained salvation. They have turned the doctrine into its opposite. Justification declares that all who believe in Jesus Christ belong at the same table... Because what matters is believing in Jesus, detailed agreement on justification itself, properly conceived, isn't the thing which should determine Eucharistic fellowship.[16]

Or, as he puts it in his commentary on Romans, 'The church's witness ... must shine out again, precisely with the message of Romans and Galatians, that in Christ there is neither Jew nor Greek, and if so then certainly neither Catholic nor Protestant.'[17]

The Reformers used the writings of Paul in their attacks on medieval Roman Catholic merit theology. But of course Wright, with the rest of the NPP, denies that Paul was opposing a merit-based theology — attempting to earn salvation by one's good works. Rather, Paul was opposing those who used the law to exclude others. Justification says that none are excluded who believe in Jesus. (This, of course, begs the question of what it means to 'believe in Jesus', but we will return to that, as well as to Wright's definition of 'faith', later.)

With that background, we now turn to our interaction with Wright's views. We begin with his understanding of the world-view and narrative structure of first-century Judaism.

THE FIRST-CENTURY JEWISH BACKGROUND: WORLD-VIEW AND STORY

According to Wright, the New Testament must be read in the light of first-century Judaism, and especially the 'worldview' that was prevalent among most Jews. World-views, Wright says, are the presuppositional, precognitive 'grid through which humans perceive reality'.[18] They are, in fact, the 'pre-theoretical point of view [which] is itself a necessary condition for any perception and knowledge to occur at all'.[19] World-views come to expression in the interacting function of four elements: story, symbols, basic questions and answers, and praxis (a way of being in the world). All four are equally important in expressing world-views, but Wright treats 'story' as more equal than the others.

Wright asserts that 'human writing is best conceived as the articulation of worldviews, or, better still, *the telling of stories which bring worldviews into articulation*'.[20] He states that 'all world-views contain an irreducible narrative element'. Stories are 'a basic constituent of human life', not there simply to illustrate some fact, principle or abstract truth. In fact, story is prior to, and more fundamental than, proposition and idea:

> ... worldviews, the grid through which humans per-ceive reality, emerge into explicit consciousness in terms of human beliefs and aims, which function as in principle debatable expressions of worldviews. The stories which characterize the worldview itself are thus located, on the map of human knowing, at a more fundamental level

than explicitly formulated beliefs, including theological beliefs.[21]

According to Wright, the three key ideas of the first-century Jewish 'worldview' were monotheism, election and eschatology. But the themes at the heart of the Jewish 'story' were creation and covenant. He states that creation and covenant are 'the two interlocking themes which stretch from one end of Paul, and indeed of the Bible, to the other'.[22] They are 'at the heart of Judaism' and were 'always central for Paul'.[23] Each theme was there to solve the problem of the other one. God's covenant with Israel was primarily to solve the problem of sin and evil in creation. Creation was invoked to solve problems within the covenant.[24] Thus we will organize our critique of Wright's narrative interpretation of Paul around these two themes.

1. Creation

Wright's depiction of the basic Jewish and Pauline 'story' begins with creation. A good, powerful God created a good world. Sin perverted that world. God's goal, then — the end of the story if you will — is to solve the problem of creation and to re-establish God's wise rule over it. Wright depicts this basic story diagrammatically as follows:

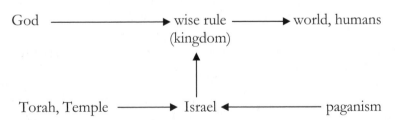

The top line indicates that God's plan is to establish his wise rule, or kingdom, over the world (creation itself) and over all people. Israel is the means that God will use to accomplish this. Israel is aided in her task by God's Word, commandments and covenant ('Torah'), as well as God's presence among his people and provision of sacrifice for sin ('Temple'). The problem is that paganism, the enemy, has invaded Israel and is keeping her from fulfilling her God-ordained task.

As we come to the first century, then, Israel finds herself in a position where she is unable to carry out her mission. Therefore, before God can rescue the world, he must first rescue his ordained servant. Thus the diagram, though similar, is altered to reflect Israel's story and her hopes in the first century:

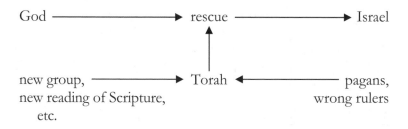

The first line shows the basic situation that God must rescue Israel. In first-century Judaism, this was by and large through Torah — primarily through faithful obedience and loyalty to Torah. As Israel — or the proper group within Israel — was faithful in upholding Torah, this would lead to deliverance, either because God responds to his people's faithfulness, or through some other means. The bottom left is indicative of the fact that first-century Judaism had a number of factions, each claiming to be the faithful remnant who upheld the covenant. The bottom right reveals the basic problem — namely, that the wrong rulers are in power. The great hope of Israel is that God would defeat the enemies, rescue and vindicate his people and establish his rule over the nations.

The four elements of world-view (story, symbols, praxis, questions and answers) reflect this narrative understanding that Israel is in exile, longing for release in order to be what God chose her to be. The stories contained in the book of Daniel were especially important for first-century Jews,

particularly chapter 7, with its vision of the 'son of man' —
Israel, the true humanity — being exalted above the beasts,
the nations who oppose God and oppress his people. The
symbols and praxis mostly revolve around Temple and Torah.
The four basic questions were these:

> 1. Who are we? We are Israel, the chosen people of
> the creator god.
> 2. Where are we? We are in the holy Land, focused
> on the Temple; but paradoxically, we are still in exile.
> 3. What is wrong? We have the wrong rulers: pagans
> on the one hand, compromised Jews on the other...
> 4. What is the solution? Our god must act again to
> give us the true sort of rule, that is his own kingship ...
> and in the meantime Israel must be faithful to his cov-
> enant charter.[25]

According to Wright, this first-century Jewish framework
is foundational for Paul and the rest of the New Testament
writers. The basic structure remains the same, even as it is
transformed and infused with new content. Wright's depiction of the early Christian 'worldview', in answering the four
questions listed above, is telling:

> Who are we? We are a new group, a new movement,
> and yet not new, because we claim to be the true people
> of the god of Abraham, Isaac and Jacob, the creator of
> the world... Where are we? We are living in the world
> that was made by the god we worship, the world that
> does not yet acknowledge this true and only god...
> What is wrong? The powers of paganism still rule the
> world... What is the solution? Israel's hope has been
> realized; the true god has acted decisively to defeat the
> pagan gods, and to create a new people, through whom
> he is to rescue the world from evil. This he has done
> through the true King, Jesus, the Jewish Messiah... The

process of implementing this victory, by means of the same god continuing to act through his own spirit in his people, is not yet complete. One day the King will return to judge the world, and to set up a kingdom which is on a different level to the kingdoms of the present world order.[26]

There is much to appreciate in Wright's depiction of the New Testament outlook. The biggest problem, however, is that it tells only part of the story and thus distorts the whole.

Focusing on the answers to questions 3 and 4 above, we can agree that for Paul and the New Testament writers *one problem* is that the powers of paganism still rule the world. The church is to do battle against the spiritual forces of darkness in the heavenly realms. The forces of darkness are the enemy of the church. But what this 'storied' approach to the New Testament fails to grapple with adequately is that New Testament writers are not preoccupied with their own problem. They are focused on the problem of the world and God's solution to that problem.

The primary problem for Paul in seeking to carry out his task as the 'apostle to the Gentiles' is that *God is the enemy.* Human beings in their sin are cut off from God. They have become God's enemies (Rom. 5:9-10; 11:28). This was one of the things that Saul of Tarsus came to recognize on the road to Damascus when the 'Lord' said to him, 'Saul, Saul, why are you persecuting me?' Saul had believed that he was among 'true Israel', zealous for Torah, devoted to doing God's work. He was God's friend. But he came to see that he was God's enemy, as is true of all Jews who reject Christ (Rom. 11:28). The solution to the problem, then, is that individual human beings must be reconciled to God, and this happens only as they repent of sin and trust Christ to save them. When they do this, they are 'justified', declared to be in right relationship with God, and thus have peace (reconciliation) with God (Rom. 5:1).

Paul clearly looked for the restoration of creation (Rom. 8:18-25). He also certainly desired the church to be one family of all nations, in fulfilment of God's promise to Abraham. In fact, we know of *no* reputable, traditional Reformed interpreter who denies these things. But God builds his church by calling individuals out of their sin and alienation to be reconciled to himself. God's new creation begins with the transformation of individual hearts: '… if anyone is in Christ, he is a new creation. The old has passed away; behold, the new has come' (2 Cor. 5:17).

Wright consistently — and frustratingly — states only two options for how we are to view salvation: salvation is either an ahistorical rescue *from* the world (the position he rejects, and which, evidently, he sees as being that of the Reformed and evangelical camps), or salvation is the transhistorical redemption *of* the world.[27] But this is both a distortion of the traditional Reformed view and a dangerous dichotomizing of the biblical world-view.

Salvation in the New Testament is first and foremost salvation from the wrath of God (cf. Rom. 5:9; 1:18; 1 Thess. 5:9; Eph. 2:1-3). Human beings were created to glorify and delight in God. This requires fellowship with God, the precise state that Adam and Eve enjoyed. But their sin ruptured that fellowship. God had warned them, 'in the day that you eat of [the tree of the knowledge of good and evil] you shall surely die' (Gen. 2:17). This death, of course, was not immediate physical death — they lived on earth many years after their sin. It was primarily spiritual death — separation from God, under God's condemnation — which was also the cause of later physical death.

If there is a fundamental 'story' for Paul, *this* is it. If there is a basic narrative structure, it centres on a holy God who cannot countenance human sin and who must punish it, but who also makes a way for human beings to be reconciled to the holy God whom they have offended, and with whom they have lost fellowship because of their sin. If the 'story' is about redeeming creation, it focuses on the climax and crown of God's creation, man, who was created in God's image to bring glory to God. Sin has marred that image. Thus God is glorified primarily as man is restored to a right relationship with God and finally transformed into a 'glorified' state in the image of Christ, who is the image of God (not a simple restoration of what was lost in the Fall, as Wright asserts[28]).

Wright's story begins with the Creator God who is at work restoring his good creation and reasserting his lordship over that creation. We agree that this is basic to the biblical account. But there is a more basic story that begins not with *what God has done* but with *who God is* — the holy God who does all things for his own glory. Wright consistently asserts that the Reformed emphasis on individual salvation is ahistorical, individualistic and human-centred. We beg to differ. God's transformation of sinful man, the crown of God's creation originally created in the image of God to glorify God, into the glorified image of Christ is the most God-centred and God-glorifying of all approaches to biblical teaching.

The problem with Wright's narrative approach (as with all narrative interpretations of Scripture) is that a single 'story' or 'narrative' cannot adequately encompass the complexities in the biblical record. Wright is often critical of the Reformed approach to Paul, arguing that it imposes its own theological agenda on the biblical text. But he himself has imposed his own defective narrative structure on the biblical text, and this has led him to his faulty conclusions — both in his reading of Paul and in his dangerous theological formulations (we will return to these later).

To put it differently, Paul did not simply adapt a first-century Jewish world-view with redefined hopes and beliefs. He radically transformed it by looking at the coming of Messiah Jesus in the light of the totality of Scripture and the fundamental human problem in the light of the nature of God. The key elements in Wright's narrative reading of Paul — Christ's lordship over the world, the transformation of all creation, Paul's missionary emphasis and the problem of paganism and the powers of darkness — are all important aspects of Paul's thought and ministry. But by making these the heart of Paul's 'story', Wright distorts the whole. When Christ returns, he will complete his 'new creation', making a new heaven and new earth. Until that time, Paul's ministry is about calling individual sinners to be reconciled to God, thus making them a new creation 'in Christ' (2 Cor. 5:17).

One final point before we move on to examine Wright's understanding of covenant: he is explicit in his belief that one key element of the New Perspective on Paul is its narrative approach to the New Testament.[29] Yet this is precisely one of its major defects. While narrative approaches can have some limited benefit, they cannot adequately deal with the nuances and the varieties of ways in which the biblical writers approach the Old Testament and interpret God's redemptive work in the world. Thus they distort the whole.

If Paul is read simply from Wright's narrative framework — namely, that God is re-establishing his rule over creation, defeating the pagan enemies that have usurped his authority — then salvation would logically simply be the redemption of the world and justification would be vindication. But that is not the entire story, nor does it grasp what Paul sees as the fundamental human problem. For Paul, the heart of the story is that man, created in the image of God and for fellowship with God, has rebelled against God's authority. He is in a state of alienation from God. In Christ God has acted to bring about reconciliation and restore man to a right relationship with himself. Thus salvation and justification have primarily a vertical dimension, and deal with the restoration of individual sinners to the God they have offended — though not in an ahistorical way and not to the exclusion of the restoration of all creation.

These aspects of Paul's teaching will become clearer as we turn to Wright's view of covenant.

2. Covenant

According to Wright, God's way of dealing with the problem of sin and rebellion in creation was to enter into a covenant with Abraham and his descendants. He states that 'God's way of putting the world right is precisely through his covenant with Israel.'[30] For Wright, this covenant is at the heart of the biblical story. The covenant will lead to the new creation and to the restored cosmos.

One of the helpful aspects of Wright's work (and indeed of the NPP generally) is that he highlights the importance of covenant in the Bible. This focus on the biblical covenants has been a hallmark of Reformed theology. To many in the Reformed camp, the emphasis on covenant has made Wright appear to be an ally. But when we look more closely at how he defines and describes 'covenant', it is clear that his covenantal approach is decidedly different from the traditional Reformed one. Significantly, his narrative approach to the Bible leads to reductionism, distortion and a failure to appreciate the nuances in the biblical depiction of the covenants. This in turn leads to serious theological error.

We will begin with Wright's own statement of what he means when he uses the term 'covenant': 'Here we have it: *God's single plan, through Abraham and his family, to bless the whole world*. That is what I have meant by the word *covenant* when I have used it as shorthand in writing about Paul.'[31] While this might be what Wright means by 'covenant', it is not what the Bible means by 'covenant'. In Scripture, a covenant is not a 'plan'. A covenant is a treaty, a way of securing promissory relationships. A covenant establishes two parties in a binding relationship with one another.

Thus, when God makes a covenant with his people, he is entering into a binding relationship with them. This is crucial to understand from the outset because Wright treats the question of how a sinner can be right with God as a later medieval imposition on the biblical text. But being in a living, saving relationship with the God of the universe is at the heart of the biblical covenants.

This will become clearer as we examine the following assertion of Wright: '... the point of the covenant always was that God would bless the whole world through Abraham's family.'[32] The key phrase here is *the point of the covenant*. It is indisputable that part of God's plan is to bring about a renewed cosmos, a new heaven and new earth, and to bless all the nations. The last book of the Bible clearly anticipates this, describing 'a great multitude that no one could number, from every nation, from all tribes and peoples and languages, standing before the throne and before the Lamb' (Rev. 7:9). This is integral to God's plan, an essential aspect of his covenant purposes. But to refer to this as *the point* of the covenant is questionable and reductionist.

If anything, the purpose of God's covenant is to gather a people for himself so that he might be glorified in and through them. The constant promises of the covenant are, 'I will be your God and you will be my people,' and 'I will be with you.' God's presence with his people means that he reveals his glory in their midst, and their primary responsibility is to worship and honour God (cf. Exod. 20 – 40). Israel is indeed called to be a light to the nations. But, just as significantly, Israel is called to be set apart from the nations on whom God will bring judgement. In fact, one of the key themes in the Israelites' taking possession of the promised land is the annihilation of the nations dwelling there, God sometimes saying that he will do it and sometimes instructing the Israelites that they must do it. The only way for anyone to escape God's wrath is by finding refuge in the God of Israel.

Wright consistently appeals to God's covenant with Abraham in Genesis 12 and 15. But when we look carefully at what God says to Abraham in those chapters, it is clear that the weight of God's promises is not on the blessing of the nations. Rather, the focus is on settling Abraham and his descendants in the land, making of Abraham a great nation and bringing judgement on the nations that oppose God's people:

> Now the LORD said to Abram, 'Go from your country and your kindred and your father's house to the land that I will show you. And I will make of you a great nation, and I will bless you and make your name great, so that you will be a blessing. I will bless those who bless you, and him who dishonours you I will curse, and in you all the families of the earth shall be blessed' (Gen. 12:1-3).

> After these things the word of the LORD came to Abram in a vision: 'Fear not, Abram, I am your shield; your reward shall be very great.' But Abram said, 'O Lord GOD, what will you give me, for I continue childless, and the heir of my house is Eliezer of Damascus?' And Abram said, 'Behold, you have given me no offspring, and a member of my household will be my heir.' And behold, the word of the LORD came to him: 'This man shall not be your heir; your very own son shall be your heir.' And he brought him outside and said, 'Look towards heaven, and number the stars, if you are able to number them.' Then he said to him, 'So shall your offspring be' (Gen. 15:1-5).

> Then the LORD said to Abram, 'Know for certain that your offspring will be sojourners in a land that is not theirs and will be servants there, and they will be afflicted for four hundred years. But I will bring judgement on the nation that they serve, and afterwards they shall come out with great possessions. As for yourself, you shall go to your fathers in peace; you shall be buried in a good old age. And they shall come back here in the fourth generation, for the iniquity of the Amorites is not yet complete.'

... On that day the LORD made a covenant with Abram, saying, 'To your offspring I give this land, from the river of Egypt to the great river, the river Euphrates, the land of the Kenites, the Kenizzites, the Kadmonites, the Hittites, the Perizzites, the Rephaim, the Amorites, the Canaanites, the Girgashites and the Jebusites' (Gen. 15:13-21).

The promises in these passages focus on Abraham's own seed becoming great and taking possession of the land of Canaan. There is one brief reference to the nations being blessed in Abraham. But even more prominent is the theme of God's judgement on the nations — explicit in Genesis 15:14, implicit in 15:16-21, since the nations who dwell in the promised land are to be wiped out.

In Genesis 17 God says to Abraham, 'Behold, my covenant is with you, and you shall be the father of a multitude of nations' (v. 4). Indeed, God made a great people of Ishmael's descendants and later of Esau's. But these nations became the enemies of God's people and were the ultimate recipients of God's *judgement*. As God says later in Genesis 17, 'As for Ishmael, I have heard you; behold, I have blessed him and will make him fruitful and multiply him greatly... I will make him into a great nation. But I will establish my covenant with Isaac...' (vv. 20-21). The emphasis here is not on unity of nations in the covenant with Abraham, but *separation*. The descendants of one are God's people; the descendants of the other are the enemies of God, destined for judgement: 'Jacob I loved, but Esau I hated' (Rom. 9:13; cf. Mal. 1:2-3). To put it differently, the blessing of nations through Abraham in this context has nothing to do with a restored creation. Rather, the blessing is temporal and numerical only; their ultimate end is destruction.

On closer examination, then, the covenant with Abraham has a completely different tenor from what Wright depicts. Instead of a narrative about creation's restoration and the unity of the nations — the grid through which Wright reads everything — the narrative is about God's gathering to himself a people and bringing judgement on those who do not belong to him — all to his glory!

Furthermore, both Old and New Testaments also make clear that all of ethnic Israel are not the true people of God. There is a remnant within ethnic Israel who belong to the true Israel (Rom. 9:6; 11:1-7). God's holy nation is made up of individuals whom he has called to himself — out of Israel and out of the nations. Individual salvation — i.e., how can a sinner be right with God? — is not a later medieval imposition on the biblical text. It is at the heart of the biblical 'story'. And Genesis 15:6 answers that question: '[Abraham] believed the LORD, and he counted it to him as righteousness.' 'Ungodly' Abraham (Rom. 4:5), like all sinners, was justified by faith. If God's covenants focus on a relationship with God, then a critical question is, how can one be in that relationship?

Wright's failure to read the biblical covenants properly and to appreciate the nuances in each of them is evident in a number of other ways also. For instance, while recognizing the presence of covenants (plural), he continually refers to 'the covenant' (singular). Classic Reformed covenant theology has used the singular to refer to the 'covenant of grace'. But it has also recognized different 'covenants' (plural) within the larger covenant of grace and the differing role that each of those covenants plays. We see none of this in Wright. Rather, he flattens the covenants and paints with a broad brush in places where the biblical record requires carefully nuanced distinctions.

For instance, Wright fails to see the unique place and purpose of the Mosaic covenant. Paul's argument in Galatians 3 – 4 hinges on a carefully nuanced distinction between 'two covenants' — that with Abraham and that with Moses. In one sense, Paul affirms a clear continuity between these covenants — the law (the Mosaic covenant) is not contrary to God's promises (given in the covenant with Abraham). Yet the basis for this affirmation is that the law cannot give life: 'For if a law had been given that could give life, then righteousness would indeed be by the law' (Gal. 3:21).

Wright, however, states, 'The original intention of the Torah was to give life, presumably to those to whom it was given, i.e. Israel...'[33] He asserts that 'the original intention of the Torah' has failed, and requires a 'fallback' plan.[34] But the larger biblical picture is that the law perfectly fulfils God's purpose for it. The law was never intended to give life. Paul asks, 'Why then the law? It was added because of transgressions' (Gal. 3:19). For Wright, this means 'to deal with transgressions'. But since when Paul uses 'transgression' the word means breaking a known command of God, this verse cannot mean that God gave the law to deal with transgressions that already existed. The meaning must be 'to bring forth', or better, 'to show forth', the depth of human sin in transgressing the law of God. As Paul says elsewhere, 'through the law comes knowledge of sin' (Rom. 3:20). One vital purpose of the law was to show God's people their sin and lead them to Christ (Gal. 3:24).

Another important biblical aspect of the Mosaic covenant which is absent in Wright's exegesis is its typological function. This is especially clear in how he treats old-covenant sacrifices. In his view (along with that of the rest of the NPP), a clear evidence of the grace of the old covenant is that God gave sacrifices to deal with sin. In fact, for Wright sacrifices are evidence that God did not require perfect obedience to the law, since they are God's provision for sin. From a biblical perspective, however, the sacrifices of the Mosaic covenant did not take away sin (Heb. 10:1-4). They were merely a reminder of sin, pointing to the only sufficient sacrifice, Jesus Christ.

This 'typological' purpose of the Mosaic covenant is, of course, not prominent in Jewish thinking. So it makes sense that it is absent in the theology of Wright, who reads the New

Testament largely through a first-century Jewish lens. While first-century Jewish writings are an important background for understanding the New Testament, it is always the larger biblical picture that is primary for understanding the Bible. Scripture interpreting Scripture is a central tenet of the Reformation. The *Westminster Confession of Faith* states,

> The infallible rule of interpretation of Scripture is the Scripture itself: and therefore, when there is a question about the true and full sense of any Scripture (which is not manifold, but one), it must be searched and known by other places that speak more clearly (1.9).

As we showed in the previous chapter, the Mosaic covenant was clearly gracious, rooted in God's redeeming work and a continuation of the covenant made with Abraham. Thus it was part of the larger covenant of grace. But its unique role within that covenant was to show God's demand and human inability to meet it. In this sense, not only does the Mosaic covenant point forward to Christ, but it also looks back as a reminder of God's 'covenant of works' with Adam.

Perhaps the biggest deficiency in Wright's 'covenant theology' is his failure to factor the covenant of works into his depiction of the biblical story. Although he recognizes the impact of Adam's sin, God's covenant with Adam, as well as the significance of that covenant and its stipulations, plays absolutely no part in his discussion of the biblical covenants. Wright does not treat the covenant with Adam on its own terms. Instead, he merges Adam with Israel.

Drawing on first-century Jewish literature that links Adam and Israel, he traces the narrative of God's 'servants', beginning with Adam, who failed in his task. In response, God called and set apart his second servant, Israel. According to Wright, Israel became corporate Adam, 'God's true humanity'.[35] Where the first Adam and then Israel failed, Israel's

Messiah succeeded. For Wright, Christ was the second Adam only as he became the representative Israelite. He states, 'The theological structure I have proposed shows that Servant-christology and Adam-christology belong well together, and cannot be played off against each other. Both, in the last analysis, are *Israel*-christologies.'[36] In other words, instead of seeing Adam and Christ as the corporate representatives of those who belong to them ('in Adam ... in Christ', 1 Cor. 15:22), Wright connects them through Israel.

Once again, then, Wright's 'story', in which Israel is at the centre, solving the 'problem' of evil in the world, is the grid through which he reads the covenant with Adam. This is problematic, if for no other reason than that God's covenant with Adam came long before the covenant with Abraham. More significantly, it misses the uniqueness of the covenant with Adam.

By omitting the covenant with Adam from his covenantal presentation of the Bible, Wright does not wrestle with the nature of God's demand, the biblical emphasis on the result of Adam's sin, or the totality of what is required to remedy the problem caused by that sin. God's covenant with Adam teaches us that God demands perfection. The covenant itself emphasizes that the result of Adam's sin is death — eternal condemnation and alienation from God. And the remedy, because the covenant of works is rooted in the character of God, comes not through Israel being a light to the nations, but through the coming of one who not only died to sin, but who perfectly kept God's law and gives his perfect righteous-ness to those who believe in him.

Israel, in short, was never intended to be the 'physician' who brought the cure to the fundamental problem of human-ity — alienation from God. This is the problem that Wright continually glosses over, preferring instead to present evil and chaos in the world as the central issue. But what he sees as the main problem is simply the outworking of a more significant one. In one sense he is correct that Jesus came as the true

Israelite, the embodiment of the hopes and dreams of his people, the one who was victorious 'in the wilderness' (and everywhere else!) where Israel failed. But in another sense, to undo the principal effects of Adam's sin, Christ was also the second Adam who perfectly obeyed where the first Adam failed.

God's covenant with Adam was made in a state of paradise, where one sin brought the curses of the covenant and plunged all humanity into sin and misery. In God's covenant with Israel, particularly the Mosaic covenant, the ultimate curse of the covenant — exile and being driven from the presence of God in his sanctuary — came only after years and countless instances of sin. When we merge these, as Wright does, we miss the heart of the biblical 'story'.

God's covenant with Abraham and his descendants was intended first and foremost to solve the fundamental problem of alienation from God that was the result of Adam's sin. The covenant of grace meant that God was calling to himself a people, to be in relationship with them, to have fellowship and communion with them, to dwell in their midst, to be their God and take them for his own people. Israel was indeed also called to be a light to the nations. Here Wright is very helpful. But by making this primary, he has distorted the whole.

Already we can see how Wright's lack of care in approaching the covenants fails to appreciate biblical nuances and leads to significant theological errors. A failure to understand the Mosaic covenant in its proper biblical context will inevitably lead to either legalism or antinomianism. A failure properly to understand God's covenant of works with Adam misses God's demand for perfect obedience and undercuts the believer's confidence and assurance in the finished work of Christ.

Ironically, Wright takes those in the Reformation tradition to task for imposing systematic theology on the biblical text and for asking questions of the text that it was not attempting to answer. But he himself has essentially done what he accuses others of doing. He has imposed his own grid, coming primarily through the lens of first-century Judaism, and interprets Paul through his own systematic reading of the biblical 'story'. Does Wright's jigsaw puzzle, with Paul being interpreted through the lens of selected writings from first-century Judaism, fit together better than the historic Reformed reading that interprets one part of inspired Scripture in the light of the rest of inspired Scripture? We think not.

Wright has consistently accused his critics of not understanding what he is saying with regard to justification because they have failed to read him in the light of the larger narrative structure that he puts forth. Having examined that narrative structure, and found it wanting, we are now in a position to examine his teaching on justification.

6.

JUSTIFICATION BY FAITH: THE BIBLICAL DOCTRINE

In the previous chapter, we saw that N. T. Wright's understanding of justification is tied to his narrative approach to the Bible, which views the biblical story as God's work redeeming his creation from the sin and evil that resulted from Adam's fall. In that context, salvation is the rescue of God's people within history and for the world. Justification is the vindication of God's people over their enemies.

Yet we also saw that Wright's version of the biblical narrative is a truncated one that doesn't tell the whole story. In particular, there is no place in his narrative structure for seeing the main storyline as being the enmity between God and man because of humanity's sin, nor for seeing salvation first and foremost as being saved from God's wrath. The reason for this is that Wright sees the New Testament as adapting a first-century Jewish world-view that focuses on Israel's plight and desire for rescue from her enemies. His storyline really begins in earnest with God's covenant with Abraham.

Paul's world-view, in contrast, goes back to God's covenant with Adam, and focuses on the primary result of Adam's sin: '... in the day that you eat of it you shall surely die.' Death — spiritual death, condemnation, alienation from God — is the real plight of mankind. In Christ, for those who are united to Christ by faith, the effects of the Fall have been overcome.

God's wrath has been turned away, the guilty are declared to be righteous, and eternal life glorifying God and in communion with God — in a garden that is also a city! (Rev. 21 – 22) — are the result.

Paul did not simply pick up and adapt the first-century Jewish world-view, as Wright claims. He radically rethought his own Jewish training and hopes in the light of the total biblical story! Or, perhaps better, divine revelation in and through him proved a better option than human stories. It was God's revelation, not Paul's own meditation, which led him to rewrite the basic storyline and world-view of his upbringing.

This leads to a very different understanding of justification from the one presented by Wright. Looking closely at Wright's narrative structure, as we did in the previous chapter, is vital to understanding his depiction of justification and how he arrived there. But in the present chapter we will focus on his formulations regarding justification itself. We will see that when the whole Bible is understood properly in its own right — not through a faulty first-century Jewish storyline — the Reformation understanding of justification by grace alone through faith alone in Christ alone to the glory of God alone is more in line with the teaching of Paul himself.

In examining Wright's new perspective on justification, we will look at four things in particular: his understanding of the gospel; his definitions of righteousness and justification; his denial of the imputation of Christ's righteousness; and his assertion of both a present and a future justification. Before doing that, however, it will be helpful to put forward the traditional Reformed understanding of justification — which we believe to be the biblical doctrine.

JUSTIFICATION: THE TRADITIONAL REFORMED
UNDERSTANDING

The best summary of the traditional Reformed understanding of justification is found in the *Westminster Shorter Catechism*, question 33: 'Justification is an act of God's free grace, wherein he pardons all our sins, and accepts us as righteous in his sight, only for the righteousness of Christ imputed to us, and received by faith alone.' We can highlight several aspects of this succinct definition.

First, justification is *an 'act' of God's free grace*. It is not a work. It is not an ongoing process. It is a legal declaration in which God, the holy and righteous Judge, declares that sinners are forgiven and righteous in his sight. This declaration, furthermore, is not the making known of what is already a reality. God's legal declaration is effectual in making individual sinners innocent in the eyes of the court. It puts them in a right relationship with God. Justification does not make them morally righteous. It declares them righteous in a legal sense. Furthermore, it is a once-for-all declaration. It is not rescinded. It is not provisional, waiting for further evidence. If God has declared you 'justified', you will never be more justified than you are right now.

Secondly, 'righteous' carries with it the meaning of *both status and moral quality*. God declares a sinner righteous — that is, in a right relationship with himself (status). Yet that declaration must be according to God's perfect standard, which of course the sinner cannot meet. Thus the sinner needs an external righteousness, a perfect righteousness that is given to him. This perfect righteousness is the clean robe that covers the sinner's righteousness, which is like filthy rags.

Thirdly, when Scripture says that we are justified by faith, it is emphasizing that we have been declared righteous *not because we ourselves are righteous*, but for another reason. Furthermore, being justified by faith does not mean that we are justified on the basis of our belief, on account of our belief, or on the ground of our own believing — that would just be another way of saying that we are justified by something we are or do. To say that we are 'justified by faith' means that faith is the instrument, or means, by which we receive God's gracious justification, a declaration based on something outside of ourselves.

Fourthly, the doctrine of justification by faith is not merely that we are justified by our faith as opposed to our works. It is not that our faith saves us rather than our works, or that our faith is the basis of our salvation, rather than our works. Rather, the doctrine of justification by faith says that we are justified by God's grace, not because of our works, *but because of Christ's work* — the saving benefits of which we receive by faith.

In other words, the reason for which God accepts us and pardons us is not found in us! It is not because we were good. It is not because we were better than others. It is not because God foresaw good works in us. It is not because God foresaw faith in us. Justification is based upon what God saw in Christ and credited to our account, which is called 'imputation'.

This is a glorious, radical truth. But, through the years, many have attempted to modify the doctrine of justification. One reason for this is, no doubt, that people cannot imagine that God would declare sinners to be righteous. It is counter-intuitive. But that is precisely what God does through Jesus Christ. Paul insists that God pardons those who don't deserve to be pardoned, declares righteous those who are unrighteous and accepts those who should not be accepted. The traditional understanding of justification by faith is that radical! Far from being an ahistorical, individualistic, human-centred doctrine, justification by faith is God-centred and God-glorifying. It exalts God, not man.

In chapter 2, we saw in Romans 3:21-26 that justification is God's answer to the problem of human sin, which deserves God's wrath and brings alienation between God and man. But Christ died for sin, bearing the punishment his people deserve and turning aside the wrath of God. Those who trust in Christ are justified by God's grace as a free gift. Human sin, which has caused all to fall short of God's glory, means that none can earn God's favour. For God to save anyone, it must be by his own provision. Furthermore, God's way of justifying sinners upholds his righteousness and justice, which demand that sin be punished. But God satisfied his justice by pouring out his wrath on his Son as a substitutionary atonement. Thus Romans 3:21-26 makes clear that justification has to do first and foremost with the vertical relationship between God and man, and the question of how a holy and just God can pardon and accept sinners.

WRIGHT ON JUSTIFICATION AND THE GOSPEL

Having laid out the traditional Reformed understanding of justification, we now turn to Wright's views. We begin by looking at the relationship between justification and the gospel. Wright explicitly states, 'By "the gospel" Paul does not mean "justification by faith".' In contrast, the Reformed tradition has maintained that the message of justification, even if the word itself is not used, is at the heart of the gospel message.

There is good reason for linking the gospel with justification. Paul uses the word 'gospel' seventy-three times in his letters, occurring in sixty-seven verses. One third of those occurrences (twenty-four) are in Romans and Galatians, the two letters that deal the most with the theme of justification. But more important than numbers is the fact that in both letters Paul expounds 'the gospel' in terms of justification by faith.

In Galatians, Paul twice refers to 'the truth of the gospel' (Gal. 2:5,14). This truth is set over against 'another gospel' — which is not a gospel at all (1:6-7). These 'gospels', in turn, are summarized as justification 'through faith' and justification 'by works of the law' (2:16; cf. 3:2,5, etc.). Paul's other letters, in addition to his speeches in Acts, indicate that his gospel contains other elements as well. For instance, the 'gospel' (1 Cor. 15:1) that he preached to the Corinthians includes the declaration 'that Christ died for our sins … was buried … was raised on the third day … that he appeared to' many of his followers, and that he reveals his grace to sinners (1 Cor. 15:3-11). But at the very least, we must say that justification by faith is essential to the gospel message.

In Romans, as commentators have historically consistently held, Paul lays out the gospel message that he had desired to preach in Rome (Rom. 1:15), but thus far had been providentially hindered from doing so. This gospel reveals the good news of 'the righteousness of God' (Rom. 1:17), as well as the bad news of the wrath of God revealed against human sin (Rom. 1:18). We will return to Romans later, but suffice it to say at this point that the gospel as portrayed in Romans proclaims that sinners, who deserve God's wrath, are justified because of God's grace and mercy through faith in Jesus Christ (Rom. 3:21-26).

To put it simply, Paul's 'gospel' contains a number of truths that are vital 'for salvation' (Rom. 1:16). These truths are closely tied together. If any element is lost, the message as a whole is lost. For instance, the statement, 'Christ died for our sins', cannot be fully comprehended without some understanding of who Christ is (would it be just as effective to say Barcley or Duncan died for our sins?), why he had to die and what our sins have to do with it all. Justification by faith, while not the totality of the gospel, is an essential component of it.

In the light of this, let's look at the entire paragraph of Wright, the first sentence of which is quoted above:

> By 'the gospel' Paul does not mean 'justification by faith'. He means the announcement that the crucified and risen Jesus is Lord. To believe this message — to

give believing allegiance to Jesus as Messiah and Lord
— is to be justified in the present by faith (whether or
not one has ever heard of justification by faith). Justification by faith is a second-order doctrine. To believe it
is both to have assurance (believing that one will be
vindicated on the last day [Romans 5:1-5]) and to know
that one belongs in the single family of God, called to
share table fellowship with all other believers without
distinction (Galatians 2:11-21). But one is not justified
by faith by believing in justification by faith, but by believing in Jesus.[1]

Here we find Wright's definition of 'the gospel': 'the
announcement that the crucified and risen Jesus is Lord', or,
as he sometimes simply puts it in shorthand, 'Jesus is Lord.'
The proclamation that 'Jesus is Lord' is indeed at the core of
the gospel message: '… if you confess with your mouth that
Jesus is Lord and believe in your heart that God raised him
from the dead, you will be saved' (Rom. 10:9; cf. 1 Cor. 12:3;
2 Cor. 4:5; and the many passages that refer to 'Jesus Christ
our Lord' or simply 'the Lord Jesus Christ'). But there is more
to it than that.

John Piper responds:

The announcement that Jesus is the Messiah, the
imperial Lord of the universe, is not good news, but is
an absolutely terrifying message to a sinner who has
spent all his life ignoring or blaspheming the God and
Father of the Lord Jesus Christ and is therefore guilty
of treason liable to execution.[2]

The quotation from Piper highlights the key difference
between Wright's view and the traditional one. If salvation is
all about God's asserting his just rule over the universe, then
the gospel can be reduced to 'Jesus is Lord'. But if the real
problem is the alienation between God and man, then the

gospel must include some account of how a rebellious traitor can be reconciled to the holy God whom he has spurned.

Galatians demonstrates the error of equating the proclamation of Christ's lordship with the gospel. Most commentators agree that the agitators of the Galatian church believed in Jesus as Lord, yet espoused 'another gospel'.[3] And Paul pronounces them accursed. Why? They preached a different gospel of justification by works of the law. Thus the gospel must include a proper account of how one can come into a right relationship with God. This leads us to look more closely at Wright on justification.

WRIGHT ON 'JUSTIFICATION' AND 'RIGHTEOUSNESS'

Justification

According to Wright, justification does not refer to God's declaration whereby one comes into a right relationship with God. It is, rather, God's declaration that someone is already 'in the right'. This is a subtle, even confusing, distinction. But it is key for understanding the difference between Wright's view of justification and the traditional Reformed view. For Wright, justification is God's vindication of those who truly belong to him, as evidenced by their having the proper badges of covenant membership. For the Christian, that badge is faith.

Justification, then, does not put someone in a right relationship with God, according to Wright. It is a declaration given for assurance, and its primary purpose is to assure all those who believe in Jesus that they are part of God's covenant people. Thus, as Wright puts it, justification is 'the great ecumenical doctrine'. Justification provides the answer to 'the question of whether Jewish Christians were allowed to eat with Gentile Christians'.[4] He continues, 'Justification declares that all who believe in Jesus Christ belong at the same table, no matter what their cultural or racial differences.'[5] Similarly, according to Wright, to be declared, or reckoned, 'righteous' means to be 'within the covenant', a member of God's covenant people. (To be 'justified' and 'reckoned righteous' essentially mean the same thing. 'Justification' and 'righteousness' are formed from the same Greek root.) Closely tied to this is Wright's definition of God's righteousness as his 'covenant faithfulness'.

In determining the meaning of any word, scholars look at two things which are inextricably tied together. The first is how the word is used elsewhere, which typically provides a range of meanings such as we find in our dictionaries or in lexicons (a resource that translates from one language to another, e.g. from Greek to English). The second is the context in which a word appears. Context includes the immediate literary context of the book itself (what does this word mean in this sentence, within this paragraph, within this particular letter?), the larger context of the totality of a writer's works, the historical context in which a writer is writing and, for biblical authors, the entire biblical context.

As we have seen, Wright believes that context supports his understanding of justification and righteousness. First and foremost for him is the first-century Jewish context in which, he argues, justification means vindication and righteousness means membership within God's covenant people. He also argues that the contexts of Paul's letters favour these meanings: '... virtually whenever Paul talks about justification he does so in the context of a critique of Judaism and of the coming together of Jew and Gentile in Christ.'[6] This leads him to assert that justification has to do more with ecclesiology than soteriology. Having dealt with these first two 'contexts' in various ways already, we will only examine them again briefly below. We will spend more time showing that the larger biblical context is especially decisive in refuting Wright's definitions.

According to Wright, his definitions of justification and righteousness are simply the way first-century Jews would

have understood them. But New Testament scholar Chuck
Hill challenges this:

> The claim to have discovered and restored [the]
> broad Jewish context is central to Wright's attempt to
> redefine justification. He essentially argues that in the
> Judaism which nurtured Paul and which Paul addressed
> throughout his ministry, justification is all about coven-
> ant membership in God's Israel. Here I think he is radi-
> cally wrong. He has certainly not established this… The
> covenant relationship may be the context in which Jews
> discussed justification, but it was the context for their
> discussion of everything!
>
> When first-century Jews talked about justification by
> God, as far as I can see (so far), it had to do with the
> last judgement, or with something in the present which
> would anticipate or approximate the last judgement,
> and it was about one's standing before God in terms of
> sin. Judgement, even by Jews, was viewed as a universal
> thing and thus as a universal human concern. Jews
> would have all sorts of advantages on that day because
> they were Jews and members of the covenant. But the
> real issue was: How are you going to escape the wrath
> of God?[7]

With regard to the context of Paul's use of justification in
his letters, we saw in chapter 2, and again in our brief exposition of Romans 3:21-26 above, that Paul's main concern is
not the Jew/Gentile question (though that is certainly present), but the question of the sinner's being right with a holy
God and being saved from his wrath. In his recent book on
justification, Wright gives us one clear example of his exegetical reading of the context of Paul's statement about justification. He claims the high ground by asserting that he reads
Galatians 2:15-21 in context, in contrast to his opponents,
who read it in the light of tradition and medieval theology.

But Wright's 'context' is Galatians 2:11-14, which leads him to assert that justification (2:15-21) has to do with table fellowship (2:11-14). However, he fails to look at verses 11-14 in the light of the flow of the larger context that leads up to them — namely, a defence of Paul's apostleship and his gospel, and an assertion of his independence from the 'pillars' (v. 9) in Jerusalem. If Galatians began at 2:11, Wright would be correct to argue that justification really is about table fellowship and the unity of Jews and Gentiles. But the larger context calls that into question.

The entire letter is set against the background of a statement about Christ's person and work in saving sinners: 'Grace to you and peace from God our Father and the Lord Jesus Christ, *who gave himself for our sins to deliver us from the present evil age*, according to the will of our God and Father' (Gal. 1:3-4, emphasis added). This statement is similar to the apostolic warning: 'Save yourselves from this crooked generation' (Acts 2:40). It is a declaration about escaping God's judgement, not about being rescued from evil enemies. This is confirmed by reading on in Galatians 1: the distortion of the gospel leads to being 'accursed' (vv. 6-9) — condemned, cut off from Christ. This is true not only for those who preach it, but also for those who accept it: 'I, Paul, say to you that if you accept circumcision, Christ will be of no advantage to you... You are severed from Christ, you who would be justified by the law; you have fallen away from grace' (Gal. 5:2,4).

Wright's assertion that being 'severed from Christ' means being cut off from the faithful community is consistent with his view, but unconvincing in the light of Paul's focus on how the Galatians received the Spirit and how they came to Christ in the first place (Gal. 3:1-5).

Righteousness

With regard to the 'righteous / righteousness' word group, most biblical scholars have not seen what Wright sees. The scholarly consensus is that these words can be used in a

variety of ways depending on the context.[8] Of course, this is
not an earth-shattering insight since we can say the same of
nearly all biblical words. But whereas most biblical scholars
see nuance and variety, Wright takes a meaning that is possible — even probable — in some contexts, and makes it
central. As he does so, he downplays (if not ignores) a key
element that has always been present in discussions about
righteousness — namely, the moral, ethical dimension.
Commentators long before medieval times have understood
God's righteousness as his moral purity, closely related to his
holiness. This is strongly supported by the biblical record.
This ethical uprightness, which transcends God's covenant
with Israel, is vital to understanding Paul and the rest of
Scripture properly.

An overview of word usage in the Old Testament reveals
that the biblical writers did not use 'righteousness' in the
sense of covenant faithfulness. Mark Seifrid has shown that
only rarely do the terms 'covenant' and 'righteousness' occur
together, in spite of their frequency. 'Covenant' occurs 283
times; 'righteousness' and its cognates occur 524 times. But
'in only seven passages do the terms come into any significant
semantic contact'.[9] If righteousness is to be defined *as* covenant faithfulness, we would expect these words to be used
together more regularly.

Furthermore, Seifrid goes on to show, 'In biblical terms
one generally does not "act righteously or unrighteously" with
respect to a covenant. Rather, one "keeps", "remembers",
"establishes" a covenant, or the like.' Of course, being faithful
to God's covenant is also to act righteously since it involves
living according to God's holy standard. Thus righteousness
and faithfulness sometimes appear together. 'Nevertheless,'
Seifrid adds, 'righteousness language is more often found in
parallel with terms for rectitude or in opposition to terms for
evil, expressing approbation or condemnation.'[10] Seifrid
summarizes as follows: 'All "covenant-keeping" is righteous
behaviour, but not all righteous behaviour is "covenant-

keeping". It is misleading, therefore, to speak of "God's righteousness" as his "covenant-faithfulness".'[11]

God's righteousness, or moral rectitude, means that he has been, and will be, faithful to his covenants. But 'God's righteousness' cannot be reduced to 'covenant faithfulness'.

An examination of some key biblical passages

We now turn our attention to some key passages.

Genesis 15:6 is critical in Paul's thought: Abraham 'believed the LORD, and he counted it to him as righteousness'. Wright understands righteousness here to mean 'covenant member-ship'.[12] In his opinion, this verse is 'proleptic, referring for-ward to the covenant ceremony about to take place' in Genesis 15:7-21. He specifically denies that righteousness means 'a particular type of moral goodness ... that would earn people membership in the covenant'. Thus, for Wright, the covenant ceremony that follows the pronouncement in Genesis 15:6 determines what it means for 'righteousness' to be reckoned to Abraham. Abraham's righteousness is equiv-alent to 'covenant membership'.

But this understanding of righteousness is clearly not the most natural reading. The most natural reading is determined by the use of the 'righteous / righteousness' word-group in the immediate context. Before and after chapter 15 it clearly refers to upright action or conformity to a moral standard. Noah is called 'a righteous man, blameless in his generation' (Gen. 6:9). Although God later entered into a covenant with Noah, this statement is not made in the context of a coven-ant. Noah is morally upright, blameless. His blameless life is especially striking in view of the wickedness of the rest of mankind: 'I have seen that you are righteous before me in this generation' (Gen. 7:1).

After Genesis 15, the next time 'righteous / righteousness' is used is in *Genesis 18*. The context is God's destruction of Sodom and Gomorrah. First, Yahweh determines to reveal his plan to Abraham, saying, 'For I have chosen him, that he

may command his children and his household after him to
keep the way of the LORD by doing righteousness and justice,
so that the LORD may bring to Abraham what he has promised him' (v. 19). Then, Abraham pleads on behalf of the
'righteous', who are clearly distinguished from those who act
wickedly (vv. 23-32; cf. also Gen. 20:4, NKJV). Thus Brian
Vickers' assessment is accurate that righteousness 'is typically
connected to actions that one should do'.[13]

In context, then, to be declared 'righteous' does not mean
to be 'within the covenant'. Rather, it means to be reckoned
to have kept God's moral standard. In Scripture, sometimes
there is a one-to-one correlation between righteous actions
and the reckoning of righteousness. This is true, for example,
of Phinehas, whose righteous act was 'counted to him as
righteousness' (Ps. 106:31). In the case of Abraham, however,
his faith is counted, or reckoned, as righteousness.[14]

Brian Vickers puts it this way:

> What does it mean for God to declare Abraham's
> faith as righteousness? Simply put, it means that a dec-
> laration that would normally be declared on the basis of
> what one does has been granted on the basis of faith. In
> this way 'righteousness' refers to a status declared by
> God. By faith, Abraham stands before God as one who
> has fulfilled every standard and condition expected by
> God... The surprising turn in the story is that 'right-
> eousness', typically associated with what one does, is
> here declared on one who believes.[15]

We find this meaning of righteousness within the context
of the Mosaic law. In Deuteronomy 6:24-25, Moses tells the
people:

> And the LORD commanded us to do all these stat-
> utes, to fear the LORD our God, for our good always,
> that he might preserve us alive, as we are this day. And

it will be righteousness for us, if we are careful to do all this commandment before the LORD our God, as he has commanded us.

Similarly, in Deuteronomy 24:13, returning before the sun sets a poor man's cloak that he has used as a pledge 'shall be righteousness for you before the LORD your God'. 'Righteousness' means keeping the law.

With this biblical background, we can now examine more closely a key verse for Wright, *Romans 1:17*, and Paul's reference to 'the righteousness of God'. According to Wright, God's 'righteousness' here is his 'covenant faithfulness'. He interprets Romans 1:17 as follows: in the announcement of the gospel ('in it'), it is revealed that God has worked and is working in Jesus Christ to fulfil his covenant with Abraham. 'The gospel message about Jesus, in other words, opens people's eyes to see for the first time that this *was what God had been up to all along*.'[16] But a careful reading of Romans indicates that either one of two alternative readings is superior to interpreting God's righteousness as his covenant faithfulness.

The first is to take 'the righteousness of God', with Wright, as a reference to God's own righteousness, but to see it as referring to his moral character, or to his upright and just way of dealing with sin. Paul returns to the theme of 'the righteousness of God' in Romans 3:21-26. There he refers to God's putting forward Christ as a 'propitiation' (v. 25), that which turns aside the wrath of God. Paul goes on to say, 'This was to show God's righteousness, because in his divine forbearance he had passed over former sins. It was to show his righteousness at the present time, so that he might be just and the justifier of the one who has faith in Jesus' (vv. 25-26). In other words, God's righteousness is revealed in the fact that he deals with sin in a righteous and just way in the death of Christ. A holy and just God cannot let sin go unpunished. But there is nothing unjust in God pouring out his wrath on Christ, who bears the punishment in place of those who have faith in him. So God 'passed over' the former sins of his people, not because he is unjust, but because he planned to deal with sin in a just way in Christ.

This reading, that 'the righteousness of God' refers to God's righteous character as revealed in his 'righteous', or 'just', way of dealing with sin, is supported by the use of the 'righteousness' word-group (Greek root, *dik-*) in Romans 1 – 3. Romans 1:32 refers to God's 'righteous decree' (*dikaiōma*) that those who practise 'unrighteousness' (1:18) deserve God's condemnation. In Romans 2:5, Paul makes mention of 'God's righteous judgement' (*dikaiokrisias*). Paul refers to 'the righteousness of God' again in Romans 3:5. Here he states that God is not 'unrighteous' to inflict his wrath on the 'unrighteousness' of human beings. As the judge of the world, God must judge justly (3:6). God is righteous and just; he must deal with sin in a righteous and just way. This interpretation is more faithful to the text than reading God's righteousness as his covenant faithfulness.

The second way to read 'the righteousness of God' is Luther's interpretation that it refers to the status or gift of righteousness that God gives to sinners who trust Christ alone for salvation. The entirety of Romans 1:17 reads as follows: 'For in it the righteousness of God is revealed from faith for faith, as it is written, "The righteous shall live by faith."' This verse has two parts that could be seen as thematically parallel. The second part is a quotation from Habakkuk 2:4. The introductory phrase 'as it is written' indicates that this quotation in some way clarifies the first part of the verse. The thematic parallels are clear:

the righteousness of God … from faith for faith
the righteous … by faith

In the quotation from Habakkuk, the words 'the righteous [one]' (*ho dikaios*) refer to the human being who receives the status of righteousness. Thus 'the righteousness of God' may refer to the righteousness that God gives to human beings.

This reading can also be supported by looking at the larger context of Romans. The predominant use of the *dik-* word-group in Romans 1 – 5 is with reference to human beings who are 'righteous' (*dikaios,* 2:13; 5:19), 'justified' (*dikaioō,* 3:24; 4:2; 5:1,9, etc.), or have 'righteousness' (*dikaiosunē*) reckoned to them (4:3,5,6,9; etc.). In Romans 5:17, Paul explicitly refers to the 'free gift of righteousness'. Thus there is good justification (no pun intended) for understanding the righteousness of God as the righteousness that God gives.

In Romans 10:3 Paul twice refers to 'God's righteousness', here in contrast with the Jews' attempt to establish their own righteousness. The contrast, God's versus their own, indicates that God's righteousness refers to 'the righteousness that comes from God'. In fact, a similar passage in Philippians 3:9, where Paul contrasts his own righteousness from the law with the righteousness 'from God', supports this reading of Romans 10:3. The language is slightly different — in Philippians Paul uses the preposition 'from' (Greek, *ek*), whereas in Romans he uses the simple genitive, which is more ambiguous (it could mean either 'of' or 'from'). Nevertheless, the parallels between the two passages are close enough to suggest that 'the righteousness of God' (Rom. 10:3, literal translation) and 'the righteousness from God' (Phil. 3:9) mean essentially the same thing — both referring to the righteousness that God gives to those who trust Christ for salvation.

To sum up, in understanding 'God's righteousness' as covenant faithfulness, Wright takes a possible meaning of righteousness in some contexts and makes it central. While a human being who is 'declared righteous' is indeed in covenant relationship with God, the status of being 'within the covenant' is not the central meaning of human righteousness. Wright's definition fails to see that 'righteous' means conformity to a moral standard. In the case of Abraham, what is usually reckoned according to what one does was reckoned to

Abraham by faith. God declared Abraham to have met his moral standard. The denial of this moral dimension, ultimately rooted in Wright's faulty view of the covenants, leads to a further error — namely, the denial of the imputation of Christ's righteousness. We turn to that now.

WRIGHT'S REJECTION OF THE IMPUTATION OF CHRIST'S RIGHTEOUSNESS

In his book, *Justification: God's Plan and Paul's Vision* (his response to John Piper), Wright derogatorily refers to Piper as 'one of an increasing number who, supposing the great Reformation tradition of reading and preaching Paul to be under attack, has leapt to its defence…'[17] Wright believes his teaching to be in line with the Reformation tradition, even though he clearly departs from it on several issues. Arguably, the clearest — and most dangerous — departure from Reformation teaching is his rejection of the doctrine of the imputation of Christ's righteousness. Indeed, the issue of whether righteousness was infused or imputed was at the heart of the Protestant/Catholic debate during the time of the Reformation.

The heirs of the Reformation have historically held that the doctrine of the imputation of Christ's righteousness is vital to the Christian faith.[18] One day before his death, J. Gresham Machen sent the following message to John Murray: 'I'm so thankful for the active obedience of Christ; no hope without it.' By 'the active obedience of Christ', Machen meant Christ's obedience to the Father while he was on earth, which is then imputed to those who trust Christ alone for salvation. The reason he asserted, 'No hope without it,' is that, because God demands perfect obedience to his law (seen originally in the covenant of works with Adam and highlighted again in the Mosaic covenant), what human beings need is not just to have their sins forgiven; rather, they also need a righteousness to present to God in order for God to declare them to be 'righteous'. Since even our best righteousness is 'like filthy rags' (Isa. 64:6, NKJV), the only righteousness that meets God's standard is the perfect righteousness of Christ.

We will begin by discussing the importance of the doctrine of the imputation of Christ's righteousness. Then we will look briefly at Wright's objections to imputation, followed by a response and critique of his position. This critique will include bringing out the dangers of his rejection of this doctrine, which will lead directly into the final major section of this chapter — Wright's view of final justification according to works.

1. The importance of the imputation of Christ's righteousness

It is helpful to begin this section by quoting again question 33 of the *Westminster Shorter Catechism*: 'Justification is an act of God's free grace, wherein he pardons all our sins, and accepts us as righteous in his sight, only for the righteousness of Christ imputed to us, and received by faith alone.' The language 'imputed' is merely another way of saying 'reckoned' or 'counted', as when Scripture states, 'Abraham believed God, and it was counted to him as righteousness' (Rom. 4:3; cf. Gen. 15:6; Rom. 4:4-6,9,22). Depending on its context, it can mean to be credited to one's account (when used as a bookkeeping term) or to have a particular status as a result of the judgement rendered by the court (in legal contexts).

The basic point here is that when God makes the legal declaration 'justified', or 'righteous', in his sight (cf. Rom. 2:13 and Gal. 3:11, where 'justified' and 'righteous' are used interchangeably), his own justice requires a basis for this declaration. Since sinful human beings do not meet God's righteous standard, they can only be declared righteous by having Christ's righteousness reckoned (or imputed) to them.

The importance of this goes back to God's covenant with Adam. Adam was created without sin in an 'upright' (Eccles. 7:29) or 'righteous' state.[19] But he had not attained to a glorified and immortal state (as evidenced by the fact that he fell into sin and eventually died). To continue in fellowship with God and ultimately to attain to glorification (complete conformity to the image of God / Christ, which was God's intention in creating man in the first place), Adam needed to obey God perfectly. When he failed, not only did he die (spiritually and ultimately physically), but he also plunged all humanity into sin and death (cf. Rom. 5:12-21).

We see right from the beginning, then, that God's standard is perfection. Whether we call this a 'covenant of works', a 'covenant of creation', or use some other term, the basic fact of God's perfect requirement is established. (Thus this requirement is not a later medieval imposition on the biblical text.)

Furthermore, Genesis 3 also contains a beautiful picture of God's provision. When Adam and Eve realized that they were naked, they sewed fig leaves together and covered themselves. Yet God later makes clothing for them of animal skins. Is this because animal skin is inherently better for clothing than fig leaves? That may well be so, but it is not the main point here. The point is that God himself must cover them. This foreshadows the later Old Testament imagery that God would clothe his people with righteousness (cf., e.g., Isa. 61:10; Zech. 3:3-5). Proper clothing that covers our nakedness or our filth is God's gracious provision for his people.

Thus two things are clear in this account: the first is God's requirement of perfect obedience; the second is God's provision of clothing for his people. This is what lies behind Paul's discussion of Adam's sin and Christ's obedience/ righteousness is Romans 5. Paul does not explicitly refer here to God's perfect standard, or to humanity needing God's provision but, as Wright himself continually reminds us, when New Testament writers refer to the Old Testament, they have the entire context in mind.

As the second Adam, Christ not only needed to atone for sin, but in order to secure salvation for his elect, he had to succeed where Adam failed. He had to keep the command-ments of God perfectly. Those who are 'in Christ' — that is, who are united to Christ as their corporate representative and head — receive his righteousness and find life. Those who are 'in Adam' are subject to Adam's penalty, spiritual death and condemnation.

As an aside, two of Wright's biggest criticisms of those who disagree with his views are that they fail to understand justification in the light of the biblical doctrine of union with Christ and to see the larger covenantal structure of the Bible — so that he cries out with exasperation, 'When will it become clear to the geocentrists?'[20] (For Wright, those who hold to the 'old perspective' are akin to those who believe the sun revolves around the earth.) Over against his misunder-standing of the covenants, however, a proper view of the covenants and union with Christ requires the imputation of Christ's righteousness.

The Bible actually teaches a threefold imputation — the imputation of Adam's sin to his posterity, the imputation of the sins of Christ's people to Christ, and the imputation of Christ's righteousness to his people. Imputing something to someone does not *make* that person what is imputed. When the sins of Christ's people were imputed to Christ, Christ did not become actually sinful. So, when Christ's righteousness is imputed to his people, they do not become perfectly righteous. Legally, God declares them to be righteous ('justified'), even though they personally do not meet God's perfect standard. As those who are united to Christ and therefore receive his Spirit, they begin the process of being transformed into the image of Christ 'from one degree of glory to another' (2 Cor. 3:18). Yet even God's ongoing work of transformation will leave them in this life falling short of the glory of God.

Thus the only hope for a relationship with God is the imputation of — God's reckoning to our account — the perfect righteousness of Christ. Wright, with Roman Catholi-cism, calls this a 'legal fiction'.[21] Yet there is nothing unjust or fraudulent about God reckoning Christ's righteousness to those who are united to him, just as there is nothing fraudulent about Christ, 'who knew no sin', being sin for us (2 Cor. 5:21). In fact, because of God's holiness, his perfect standard and his just judgement, there truly is 'no hope without it'.

Wright asserts that the old and new perspectives differ in that the old sees salvation as revolving around the individual, whereas the new has a universal and cosmic emphasis. We beg to differ. The old understands the universal and cosmic dimensions of salvation. The big difference is that the old perspective upholds the honour and holiness of God — recognizing God's demand, human inability and sinfulness, and God's just judgement on human sin. The new perspective fails to honour God rightly by downplaying his standards. It is the new perspective, not the old, that is man-centred, focusing on what man accomplishes. In the old perspective man is humbled and all glory goes to God. In the new, God's glory is diminished.

Nothing less than the glory of God is at stake in the debate over imputation!

2. Wright's criticisms of the imputation of Christ's righteousness

Wright makes three primary criticisms of the doctrine of the imputation of Christ's righteousness.

a. It is not explicitly taught in Scripture

His first objection is that the doctrine is not biblical. His argument runs as follows: if the imputation of Christ's righteousness is so essential to Paul's theology, why is it not more clearly taught in his letters?

We cannot, in a book of this limited size and scope(still less in a single chapter), engage in an exhaustive response to this criticism. We point the reader to the outstanding work of Brian Vickers, *Jesus' Blood and Righteousness: Paul's Theology of Imputation*.[22] Vickers shows convincingly that the imputation of Christ's righteousness is biblical teaching, but that all of the 'ingredients' of the doctrine are not found in any one passage. When one brings together, however, the exegesis of key Pauline texts, the doctrine clearly emerges. Given the 'occasional' nature of Paul's letters, we should not expect him to set out a full-orbed presentation of any doctrine in any one place — in fact, Paul rarely (if ever) does so.

The formulation of doctrine is always the result of bringing together the exegesis of several biblical texts and coming to conclusions based both on explicit biblical teaching and 'good and necessary inference'. We believe Wright would agree that the doctrine of the Trinity is essential biblical truth. Yet nowhere does the Bible explicitly say that there is one God who exists eternally in three persons. The same is true of imputation. This emerges as we look at key passages in Paul's epistles, which we can do here only briefly.

Romans 4 uses the language of imputation — 'Abraham believed God, and it was counted to him as righteousness' — but does not explicitly say that Christ's righteousness was imputed. However, this chapter does teach us that righteousness is a gift (reckoned, not earned), that it is given to the 'ungodly' (v. 5), and that one thing (Abraham's faith) is reckoned as something that it is not (righteousness). If, as we have argued earlier (against Wright), righteousness is connected to actions that one should do, this means that God's declaration of Abraham as righteous 'means that a declaration that would normally be declared on the basis of what one does has been granted on the basis of faith'.[23] To put it differently, 'By faith, Abraham stands before God as one who has fulfilled every standard and condition expected by God.'[24] Ungodly Abraham, through faith, is granted the status of righteousness.

In *Romans 5:12-21*, Paul contrasts Adam and Christ. Here he brings out that the status of every human being is based on what their representative, Adam or Christ, has done. Adam's disobedience is contrasted with Christ's obedience/ righteousness. The fact that Paul refers both to Christ's 'act of

righteousness' (*dikaiōma,* v. 18) and to the 'free gift of righteousness' (v. 17) implies that Christ's righteousness is the gift
that sinners receive. John Piper, in fact, makes the point that
in Romans 5:15, Paul contrasts 'free gift' with 'trespass',
instead of contrasting obedience and trespass as we would
expect. This leaves the impression that the free gift that God
gives is in fact the obedience, or righteousness, of Christ. The
reference to the non-imputation of sin at the beginning of this
passage (v. 13), and perhaps the implied imputing of Adam's
sin (v. 14),[25] sets the reader up to understand Paul's argument
in the light of imputation — the 'gift' of Christ's righteousness imputed to those who belong to him.

A third key passage is *2 Corinthians 5:21*: 'For our sake he
made him to be sin who knew no sin, so that in him we might
become the righteousness of God.' This text is crucial for what
Luther called 'the great exchange' — Christ took our sin; we
receive his righteousness. Wright's interpretation of this
passage is nothing if not creative, as well as consistent in his
understanding of God's righteousness: Paul, as a minister of
the new covenant, is 'an incarnation of the covenant faithfulness of God'.[26] There are numerous problems with Wright's
interpretation, not least of which is Vickers' question: 'How
does one *become* God's faithfulness to his covenant?'[27]

This passage contains two aspects that are crucial for
interpretation. The first is the notion of believers' union with
Christ (cf. 'in Christ,' v. 17; 'in him,' v. 21). Secondly, we see a
forensic emphasis: 'in Christ God was reconciling the world
to himself, not counting ['reckoning', 'imputing' — the same
Greek word as in Romans 4:3, etc.] their trespasses against
them' (v. 19). These aspects are important as Paul moves to
verse 21, which itself highlights two things in particular:
Christ's perfect life (he 'knew no sin') and his substitutionary
death (for our sake he became sin; cf. vv. 14-15). In a forensic
sense, Christ became sin by taking our sin; he did not himself
become personally sinful. What, then, is the basis for our
becoming the righteousness of God in Christ? In a forensic

sense, we receive his perfect, sinless life. We don't become personally sinless, although as a 'new creation' (v. 17) God begins his work of making us more and more like Christ (cf. 2 Cor. 3:18).

These passages, along with verses like 1 Corinthians 1:30 (God made Christ 'our righteousness'), make a convincing case for the doctrine of the imputation of Christ's righteousness. This is especially true when seen in the light of a proper understanding of the covenantal structure of the Bible. God's perfect standard requires a perfect righteousness. But the only righteousness that meets this standard is Christ's, which becomes the believer's by virtue of his union with Christ. The believer's union with Christ, in the sense of a representational participation, in which what is legally ours becomes his and his becomes ours, rules out any notion of a 'legal fiction'.

b. It does not fit the imagery of the law court

The second criticism that Wright makes of the imputation of Christ's righteousness is that it does not fit the law-court imagery of the first century. He says:

> If we use the language of the law court, it makes no sense whatever to say that the judge imputes, imparts, bequeaths, conveys or otherwise transfers his righteousness to either the plaintiff or the defendant. Righteousness is not an object, a substance or a gas which can be passed across the courtroom. For the judge to be righteous does not mean that he or she has tried the case properly or impartially. To imagine the defendant somehow receiving the judge's righteousness is simply a category mistake... If and when God does act to vindicate his people, his people will then, metaphorically speaking, have the status of righteousness... *But the righteousness they have will not be God's own righteousness.* That makes no sense at all.[28]

Yet the language of justification necessitates the imputation of Christ's righteousness when it is considered in the
context of sinners standing before the throne of the God of
the Bible. John Piper writes:

> It is not a category mistake to speak of the defendant
> 'receiving the Judge's righteousness'. This is, in fact,
> what the language of justification demands in a law-
> court where the Judge is omniscient and just and the
> charge is 'none is [morally] righteous' (Romans 3:10).
> Of course it will jar the ordinary human categories.
> That is what the justification of the *ungodly* has always
> done — and is meant to do.[29]

c. It is 'a blind alley' that leads to 'legalism'

Wright's third criticism of the imputation of Christ's righteousness is that it is 'theologically and exegetically, a blind
alley', which actually makes the Reformed tradition that holds
to it guilty of 'legalism'.[30] This is where Wright shows most
clearly his theological confusion. He claims that 'Paul's entire
understanding of the Mosaic law is that it never was intended
as a ladder of good works up which one might climb to earn
the status of "righteousness". It was … the way of life *for a
people already redeemed*.'[31] In one sense, this is true. The Reformed tradition, as we saw in the previous two chapters, has
always emphasized the grace of the law and seen it as one
dispensation of God's covenant of grace. The giving of the
law begins with God's reminder of what he had done for his
people: 'I am the LORD your God, who brought you out of
the land of Egypt, out of the house of slavery' (Exod. 20:2).
The law is God's gracious gift to his people.

Yet the demand of the law is such that God's people
would never be able to keep it, and God told them so. The
law, then, served as a reminder (or a 're-exhibition,' as James
Buchanan calls it)[32] of the covenant of works. It was meant to
show Israel their sin and drive them to Christ. Some Israelites

had true faith (Paul refers to them as a 'remnant'). Most did not. They remained complacent in their possession of the law without recognizing that it is the doers of the law, not the hearers, who are justified (Rom. 2:13; more on this later). This is God's standard. If you are going to be saved by the law, you must do all of it.

Wright and other NPP advocates say, 'Wait, God provided sacrifices to deal with sin. You see, perfect obedience was not the requirement.' But this misses the typological function of the Mosaic law and the sacrifices under that law. Old-covenant sacrifices were meant to point forward to Christ. They never took away sin (Heb. 10:1-4). The blood of old-covenant sacrifices only achieved 'the purification of the flesh' (Heb. 9:13). The blood of Christ alone can 'purify our conscience from dead works to serve the living God' (Heb. 9:14).

The typology extends to the land. Wright incredibly asserts, '... the worst that God could threaten was that Israel would lose the promised land.' No, the worst that God threatens is hell and eternal punishment. The land served typologically to point forward to the eschatological inheritance of the new heaven and new earth. Exile for disobedience was a temporal hardship, but served as a reminder to God's people of his demand for obedience and his judgement for disobedience.

Thus it is not a 'category mistake' to uphold God's perfect standard and to insist that salvation still depends on perfect obedience to the law. Wright's charge of 'legalism' indicates once more his failure to deal adequately with the entire biblical 'story', and shows again that he is more indebted to first-century Jewish thinking than he is to the inspired Word of God.

d. The believer's union with Christ

Wright's alternative to the imputation of Christ's righteousness is the believer's union with Christ, which, he says, achieves everything that the wrong-headed traditional formula attempted to achieve. But where he goes with this is troubling and will lead us into the final section of this chapter.

Wright goes to Romans 6 to demonstrate what 'union with Christ' means. He asserts, 'It is not the "righteousness" of Jesus Christ which is "reckoned" to the believer. It is his death and resurrection. This is what Romans 6 is all about.'[33] He goes on:

> Paul does not say, 'I am in Christ; Christ has obeyed the Torah; therefore God regards me as though I had obeyed the Torah.' He says: 'I am in Christ; Christ has died and been raised; therefore God regards me — and I must learn to regard myself — as someone who has died to sin and been raised to newness of life'... The challenge to the believer — indeed, one might almost say the challenge of learning to believe at all — is to 'reckon' that this is true, that one has indeed left behind the state of slavery, that one really has come now to stand on resurrection ground (Romans 6:6-11). All that the supposed doctrine of the 'imputed righteousness of Christ' has to offer is offered by Paul under this rubric, on these terms and within this covenantal framework.[34]

While Romans 6 certainly details aspects of the believer's union with Christ, it deals more with the ongoing life of faith — walking 'in newness of life' (v. 4), not being 'enslaved to sin' (v. 6), considering ourselves 'dead to sin', and so not letting it reign in our 'mortal bodies' (vv. 11-12), presenting ourselves as slaves, not to sin, which leads to death, but to 'obedience, which leads to righteousness' (v. 16).

In other words, Romans 6 is about what theologians have called 'imparted righteousness', not imputed righteousness. It comes within the section of Romans dealing with the results of our justification — 'therefore, since we *have been justified* by faith' (Rom. 5:1, emphasis added). For Wright to say that this essentially gets at what the unbiblical doctrine of the imputation of

Christ's righteousness wanted to say, but does so in a more Pauline and biblical way, is cause for great concern. The doctrine of the imputation of Christ's righteousness says, because of our union with Christ and through faith in him, God makes a once-for-all declaration that we are justified in his sight on the basis of the perfect righteousness of Jesus Christ. Our union with Christ also means that the believer now can put sin to death and live as a slave to righteousness. But to put the two together, as Wright does, indicates that for him justification is not by faith alone in the classic Reformed sense.

Elsewhere Wright similarly appeals to Galatians 2:19-20 in an attempt to find common ground with the Reformed doctrine of imputation:

> 'I through the law died to the law, that I might live to God; I have been crucified with the Messiah; nevertheless I live; and the life I now live in the flesh I live by the faith of the Son of God who loved me and gave himself for me.' If this is what you are trying to get at by the phrase 'imputed righteousness', then I have no quarrel with the substance of it but rather insist on it as a central and vital part of Paul's theology.[35]

Again, this passage contains an aspect of union with Christ (though not as clearly in Wright's quotation, since he omits the phrase 'Christ ... lives in me'). As with the other statements in Paul's letters which speak of 'Christ in' the believer, the emphasis is on the ongoing life of faith and the believer's transformation into the image of Christ (cf., e.g., Rom. 8:10: 'But if Christ is in you, although the body is dead because of sin, the Spirit is life because of righteousness').[36] Once more, it seems as though Wright is only satisfied with the doctrine of imputed righteousness as long as it includes the idea of the believer's ongoing transformation.

Does Wright, then, believe in the doctrine of justification by faith alone? He claims that he does. And yet he is also insistent that faith includes 'faithfulness'. He states:

> One of Paul's key phrases is 'the obedience of faith'. Faith and obedience are not antithetical. They belong exactly together. Indeed, very often the word 'faith' itself could properly be translated as 'faithfulness', which makes the point just as well. Nor, of course, does this then compromise the gospel or justification, smuggling in 'works' by the back door. That would only be the case if the realignment I have been arguing for throughout were not grasped. Faith, even in this active sense, is never and in no way a qualification, provided from the human side, either for getting into God's family or for staying there once in. It is the God-given badge of membership, neither more nor less.[37]

Notice a couple things in this quotation. The first is Wright's comment that faithfulness 'makes the point just as well' as faith. The implication is that faith is faithfulness, in his opinion. Secondly, Wright seems to be saying that viewing faith as faithfulness does not smuggle works in by the back door because the works of faithfulness are 'God-given', not produced by the individual. But, as John Piper points out, the issue is not 'whether it is produced by us semi-Pelagian-like or given by God in sovereign grace. The issue is whether justification by faith really means justification by works *of any kind*, whether provided by God or man.'[38]

These aspects of Wright's teaching are closely related to one final assertion — namely, that final justification is according to works. We turn to that now.

WRIGHT'S TEACHING OF FINAL JUSTIFICATION ACCORDING TO WORKS

The Reformed tradition has typically always held that, while we are justified by faith alone, there will be a final judgement based on our works. Paul affirms this in 2 Corinthians 5:10: 'For we must all appear before the judgement seat of Christ, so that each one may receive what is due for what he has done in the body, whether good or evil.' Wright, likewise, refers to the passage above in asserting a final judgement in accordance with works:

> Paul, in company with mainstream second-Temple Judaism, affirms that God's final judgement will be in accordance with the entirety of a life led — in accordance, in other words, with works. He says this clearly and unambiguously in Romans 14:10-12 and 2 Corinthians 5:10. He affirms it in that terrifying passage about church-builders in 1 Corinthians 3. But the main passage in question is of course Romans 2:1-16.[39]

If this were all that Wright had to say about final judgement, we could affirm that he stands with the Reformed tradition on this particular issue.

The problem is that he takes a step beyond this, asserting not just final judgement according to works, but final justification according to works. He says that Paul speaks 'in Romans 2 about the final justification of God's people, on the basis of their whole life'.[40] Elsewhere he says, 'Present justification declares, on the basis of faith, what future justification will affirm publicly ... on the basis of the entire life.'[41] In other words, according to Wright, Paul does not teach present justification by faith with future judgement by works. There is both present justification and future justification, the former by faith, the latter by works.

Wright clarifies this in the following passage:

We now discover that this declaration [i.e., justifi-
cation], this vindication, occurs twice. It occurs in the
future, as we have seen, on the basis of the entire life a
person has led in the power of the Spirit — that is, it
occurs on the basis of 'works' in Paul's redefined sense.
And near the heart of Paul's theology, it occurs in the
present *as an anticipation of that future verdict*, when someone, responding in believing obedience to the call of the
gospel, believes that Jesus is Lord and that God raised
him from the dead.[42]

When Wright refers here to present justification 'as an
anticipation of that final verdict', it is possible he means that
when God declares a believer justified, the verdict is certain
and that our works are evidence of true saving faith. The
problem is that he does not make this clear and there are
indications in his writing that this is not what he means at all.

Referring to Romans 2:13, Wright states, 'The "works" in
accordance with which the Christian will be vindicated on the
last day are not the unaided works of the self-help moralist.'
Again, similarly to what we saw in the previous section, he
seems to be making a distinction between works aided by the
Spirit and the works of one who is seeking to pull himself up
by his boot-straps. The impression is that works do contribute to justification if they are Spirit-produced.

He continues:

They [the 'works' referred to in Rom. 2:13] are …
the things that show that one is in Christ; the things
that are produced in one's life as a result of the Spirit's
indwelling and operation. In this way, Romans 8:1-17
provides the real answer to Romans 2:1-16. Why is
there now 'no condemnation'? Because, on the one
hand, God has condemned sin in the flesh of Christ …
and, on the other hand, because the Spirit is at work to
do within believers what the law could not do…[43]

In other words, God's verdict, 'not guilty', is the result not just of Christ's atoning death (and certainly not because of Christ's perfect righteousness). Rather, it is the result of the Spirit's enabling believers to keep the essence of the law. As Wright says elsewhere, 'The Spirit is the path by which Paul traces the route from justification by faith in the present to justification, by the complete life lived, in the future.'[44]

In his recent book, *Justification*, Wright tries to clarify this and seems to be standing (or moving) more in the Reformed tradition on this particular issue. He says, for example:

> Paul never says that the present moral life of the Christian 'earns' final salvation... Nor does he say that one must attain moral perfection... At the same time he insists that the signs of the Spirit's life must be present: if anyone doesn't have the Spirit of Christ, that person doesn't belong to him (Romans 8:9).[45]

We agree with this. But then Wright goes on to say:

> For Paul, a stress on 'justification by faith' is always a stress on the *present status of all God's people in anticipation of the final judgement*. But when he puts this into its larger, covenantal context ... it is always filled out with talk of the Spirit.[46]

Thus far, understood in the light of Wright's own formulations and depending on what he means by 'filled out with', this may be fine. He asserts, remember, that Paul's doctrine of justification is primarily for assurance. One cannot have assurance of justification without signs of the Spirit's work in his or her life.

But then he goes on to say, 'Paul invites his hearers to trust *both* in Jesus Christ *and* in the Father whose love triumphed in the death of his Son — *and in the Holy Spirit who makes that victory operative in our moral lives and who enables us to love God in return.*' He then fires this shot across the bows: 'The trouble with some would-be Reformation theology is that it is not only insufficiently biblical. It is also insufficiently Trinitarian.'[47]

Of course, the Reformed tradition has always upheld the necessity of the Spirit's transforming work, teaching that regeneration must precede conversion. The Holy Spirit must first come and change someone's heart, making them 'born again', or 'from above' (John 3), before they can actually put their faith in Christ for salvation. The Spirit's work, in other words, is necessary both for justification and for sanctification. But the Reformed tradition also insists, in line with biblical teaching, that justification is not the result of the Spirit's work in sanctification. Wright could clearly state what he means on this issue, but thus far he has failed to do so.

All of this also needs to be seen in the light of Wright's endorsement of Jewish 'covenantal nomism', not as legalism but as a gracious pattern of religion. In 'covenantal nomism' one does not get into the covenant by good works, but one remains in it by good works. We have seen previously that, while 'covenantal nomism' is probably an adequate description of first-century Judaism, the emphasis on works to 'stay in' is itself a form of legalism. When Wright says, in the first extract quoted above in the present section, 'Paul, in company with mainstream second-Temple Judaism affirms that God's final judgement will be in accordance with the entirety of a life led — in accordance, in other words, with works,' he is saying that Paul's pattern of religion fits the covenantal nomism of first-century Judaism. If this is what Wright understands Paul to be teaching, whether or not he believes those works to be empowered by the Spirit, then his own reading of Paul is semi-Pelagian.

Wright's view of future justification according to works is based on Romans 2:13: 'For it is not the hearers of the law who are righteous before God, but the doers of the law who will be justified.' He fails, however, adequately to set this verse in its context. Paul here is dealing with the Jews who are complacent in their status because they have the law and are part of God's (old) covenant people. But Paul makes the point that having the law is no advantage — and this is so for two reasons. First, both Jews and Gentiles will be judged impartially and justly: '… all who have sinned without the law will also perish without the law, and all who have sinned under the law will be judged by the law' (Rom. 2:12). Secondly, the Jews have no advantage because even the Gentiles in a sense have the law — the 'work of the law is written on their hearts' (Rom. 2:15) as evidenced by the fact that their conscience accuses them when they break God's moral law.

What matters, then, is not having, or hearing, the law. That does not justify. It is *doing* the law that matters. In other words, Paul is saying that if you are going to claim the law as your privilege and as what will vindicate you on the Day of Judgement, then you must recognize that you need to do all of it. Paul's statement that 'the doers of the law … will be justified' is God's standard. It is not, therefore, in context meant to be a hypothetical statement (though of course it is true that no one can meet God's perfect standard). It is simply an explanation of the way God judges. You who seek justification in the law must do all that it says (a standard met only by Christ).

Romans 2:13 is the only place where Paul links future justification (in contrast to future judgement) with works. Whether Wright agrees with the interpretation presented here or not, the plausibility of this interpretation should at least give him pause in affirming an actual future justification according to works. When we hear him make comments like the following, 'I am fascinated by the way in which some of those most conscious of their Reformation heritage shy away from Paul's clear statements about future judgement according to works,'[48] it once again becomes clear that he does not understand the nuances of Reformed teaching. There will indeed be a future *judgement* according to works. But a future *justification* according to works is not biblical teaching.

CONCLUSION

This chapter has shown that Wright's definition and description of justification by faith, both in what he says and what he leaves unsaid, is a radical departure from the traditional Reformed understanding. It is not a matter of some minor tweaking based on new exegetical insights. It constitutes a new theological formulation — which also looks very much like a variety of old theological formulations. But it is not, as Wright claims, consistent with the Reformation tradition. Even with regard to Wright's assertion of *sola Scriptura* and his claim that Scripture alone is his authority, it is clear that he does not interpret Scripture in the light of Scripture, but more frequently in the light of his reading of first-century Jewish thought.

We have seen that, in Wright's formulation, he presents not just a new perspective on Paul, but a new perspective on the entire Bible. His unique 'covenant theology' (not to be confused with the covenant theology of the Reformers) — namely, *the covenant* is God's 'single-plan-through-Israel-for-the-world' — makes central what interpreters have historically understood as one implication of God's entering into a covenant relationship with Israel (blessings going to the nations; the nations coming to worship Israel's God). Instead of viewing a covenant as a binding agreement that secures promissory relationships, Wright views it as a plan. God's covenants may be part of his plan, but they are not a plan.

His unique spin on the biblical 'story' leads him in turn to understand God's righteousness as his faithfulness to his covenant, to redefine human righteousness as covenant membership and to deny the imputation of Christ's righteousness. It also seemingly leads him to adopt 'covenantal nomism' as the pattern for understanding final justification — we enter the covenant by God's grace, but we remain in the covenant by works.

We have seen through all of this that Wright flattens, reduces and either fails to recognize biblical nuances or leaves his interpretations so open-ended that it is difficult to know what he means. He often takes a potential meaning, or one aspect of a more nuanced and complex biblical concept, and makes it central (such as that the central idea of *the covenant* is God's making a single people of all the nations). But this is especially seen in his description of the gospel.

According to Wright, 'the gospel' is the declaration that Jesus is Lord. Justification by faith is not the gospel — in fact, it is not even part of the core of the gospel. It is not the message that Paul proclaimed to Gentiles. The gospel, according to Wright, is not an individualistic, self-centred message about how a sinner can be in a right relationship with a holy God. It is about God's healing the fragmentation of the world caused by human sin. 'Jesus is Lord' declares that he is Lord of all the nations. It is in this context that Wright states, '… if you start with the popular view of "justification", you may actually lose sight of the heart of the Pauline gospel; whereas if you start with the Pauline gospel itself you will get justification in all its glory thrown in as well.'[49]

We have seen, by contrast, that God's covenants are for the purpose of entering into a relationship with his people. The key phrase is, 'I will be your God, and you will be my people.' If this is the case, the key question becomes: 'What does it mean to be in relationship with a holy God?' How does one attain this status? Or, as the Philippian jailer asked, 'What must I do to be saved?' This is certainly the question that Paul faced when confronted with the crucified and resurrected Messiah and called to be the apostle to the Gentiles. If being a zealous Jew did not establish a person in relationship with God, what did? In all his zeal and 'blameless' keeping of the law, Paul was a sinner, deserving of God's wrath. So were all Jews. So were all Gentiles.

Indeed, what Wright misses is what the Bible itself emphasizes as the heart of the human problem — the fact that sin

has brought enmity between God and man, and condemnation will be the result. The warning of the covenantal curse
given to Adam was: '… in the day that you eat of it, you shall
surely die.' That death is spiritual death, the pouring out of
God's wrath. (Isn't it interesting that Wright, whose narrative
structure focuses on the horizontal redemption of this world,
and not the vertical reconciliation between God and man,
actually accuses those who place primacy on the latter as
being 'geocentrists'!)

What is needed, then, is for God to make provision for the
sin of his people. Thus Paul states in the opening verses of
Galatians that Christ 'gave himself for our sins to deliver us
from the present evil age' (Gal. 1:4). This verse, coming at the
beginning of the letter, places our focus on its central question — how can sinners be in a right relationship with God?
This is not an individualistic, self-centred message. It is a
message that includes all the nations and requires the building
of the church and living together in love, following the
example of Christ and showing Christ to the world. A false
gospel, by contrast, saves no one and results in broken
relationships: 'If you bite and devour one another, watch out
that you are not consumed by one another' (Gal. 5:15). The
true gospel unifies God's elect. A false gospel divides. The
true gospel is a message worth proclaiming to the world:
'Christ Jesus came into the world to save sinners' (1 Tim.
1:15).

The reality is this: if you hold to the new perspective on
justification, you lose the essentials of the gospel, the unity of
God's people and God's transforming message to the nations.
If you hold to the traditional view of justification (God's
declaring sinners to be in a right relationship with himself by
grace alone through faith alone in Christ alone), you get the
unity of the church and salvation to the ends of the earth —
all to the glory of God — thrown in as well!

CONCLUSION

As we conclude, we want to propose a litmus test for the teaching of the NPP. The apostle Paul, in his preaching on justification, was accused of antinomianism (Rom. 3:8). Can the same be said of the NPP? The answer is decidedly 'No'. To preach Paul's gospel, that sinners can be in a right relationship with God not by anything they have done, but only through faith in Jesus Christ and his finished work, one must run the risk of sounding antinomian. Otherwise, it is likely that the true gospel is not being preached.

Paul is clearly not antinomian. He upholds the grace and goodness of the law and makes clear that obedience to the moral law is required and is the result of true saving faith. Yet Paul preached so strongly that justification is apart from works of the law that his critics accused him of antinomianism — 'Let us do evil that good might come.' We appreciate the emphasis of the NPP on the gracious nature and the goodness of the law. In this sense the NPP is certainly a good corrective to the evangelicalism of our age which, largely owing to an overblown law/gospel contrast, downplays the place of law in the Christian life. Yet in the NPP the pendulum swings too far to the other side. No one can read N. T. Wright, for instance, and accuse him of antinomianism. Whatever Wright is saying (and we believe he still has much to clarify), law and works clearly play an important part in his formulation of justification.

The NPP claims that the evangelical church since the Reformation has misread Paul, largely as a result of the tendency of Luther and other Reformers to read his epistles in the light of their own historical situation. Luther was battling against legalism in Roman Catholicism and saw Paul as an ally, viewing his Jewish opponents similarly as legalists. Luther likewise read Paul in the light of his own individualistic concerns to escape the wrath of God due to him for his sin. But Luther's angst over sin was not Paul's. And Luther's preoccupation with the status of a sinner before a holy God was not what drove Paul's ministry — or so the NPP claims.

But a re-examination of first-century Judaism and careful exegesis reveal that the Reformers were not so very far off after all, and that it is the NPP that has been influenced unduly by the societal impulses of the present age. While there is certainly not a one-to-one correlation between the legalism of first-century Judaism and that of medieval Roman Catholicism, legalism is present in both. Legalism is endemic to sinful humanity, which worships self and fails to give glory to God (Rom. 1:21-23). What Luther encountered was simply another form of the legalism that Paul, and many Christians afterwards, fought against.

Acts 15:1 clearly demonstrates that the early church had to contend with a form of Jewish, or Jewish-Christian, legalism: 'But some men came down from Judea and were teaching the brothers, "Unless you are circumcised according to the custom of Moses, you cannot be saved."' This may not be an example of a crass form of legalism that consists of totting up merits and demerits (legalism is rarely that obvious), but it is legalism none the less. When human performance is seen as contributing to salvation, legalism is present. This seems to be the very thing that Paul was responding to in Galatians — and he believes eternal destinies are at stake. But whether one interprets Galatians against the background of Acts or not, Acts 15 gives clear evidence of a Jewish-Christian legalism causing major disruption in the early church.

We have said that to a certain extent the NPP is not all that new, in the sense that many of its basic assertions have been formulated progressively over the past 100 years. But looked at in the light of the interpretation of Paul's teaching throughout church history, the NPP is quite novel. You will not find, for instance, Wright's interpretation of righteousness or justification in any of the Church Fathers or any early interpretation of Scripture. The NPP often asserts that the reading of Paul that has come down to us since the Reformation merely reflected medieval concerns. But if you compare Luther, Calvin, *et al.*, to the earliest interpretations of the New Testament, you find striking similarities, particularly on matters that relate to the sinner's relationship to a holy God.

A good example of this can be found in *The Epistle to Diognetus*, most likely written in the second or early third century (some date it as early as the mid-120s). This letter, which scholars agree shows strong Pauline and Johannine influence, sounds decidedly 'Reformed' in its understanding of sin, justification and God's work in Jesus Christ. We quote below the entirety of chapter 9:

> And so, when he had planned everything by himself in union with his Child, he still allowed us, through the former time, to be carried away by undisciplined impulses, captivated by pleasures and lusts, just as we pleased. That does not mean that he took any delight in our sins, but only that he showed patience. He did not approve at all of that season of wickedness, but on the contrary, all the time he was creating the present age of righteousness, so that we, who in the past had by our own actions been proved unworthy of life, might now be deemed worthy, thanks to God's goodness. Then, when we had shown ourselves incapable of entering the Kingdom of God by our own efforts, we might be made capable of doing so by the power of God. And so, when our unrighteousness had come to its full term,

and it had become perfectly plain that its recompense
of punishment and death had to be expected, then the
season arrived in which God had determined to show at
last his goodness and power. O the overflowing kindness and love of God towards man! God did not hate
us, or drive us away, or bear us ill will. Rather, he was
long-suffering and forbearing. In his mercy, he took up
the burden of our sins. He himself gave up his own Son
as a ransom for us — the Holy One for the unjust, the
innocent for the guilty, the Righteous One for the unrighteous, the incorruptible for the corruptible, the immortal for the mortal. For what else could cover our
sins except his righteousness? In whom could we, law-
less and impious as we were, be made righteous except
in the Son of God alone? O sweetest exchange! O un-
fathomable work of God! O blessings beyond all expec-
tation! The sinfulness of many is hidden in the Righteous One, while the righteousness of the One justifies
the many that are sinners. In the former time he had
proved to us our nature's inability to gain life; now he
showed the Saviour's power to save even the powerless,
with the intention that on both counts we should have
faith in his goodness, and look on him as Nurse, Father,
Teacher, Counsellor, Healer, Mind, Light, Honour,
Glory, Might, Life — and that we should not be anx-
ious about clothing and food.

This early Christian writing views the New Testament as
teaching that God had a 'plan', made in conjunction with his
Son, to allow humanity to go its own way in sin and become
'incapable of entering the Kingdom of God by our own
efforts', so that God in turn might show his mercy and
kindness to sinners by sending Christ 'as a ransom for us'. In
the 'sweetest exchange', 'the Righteous One [died] for the
unrighteous' and covered their sins with 'his righteousness'.
The author asks, 'For what else could cover our sins except

his righteousness?' and goes on to assert, 'The sinfulness of many is hidden in the Righteous One, while the righteousness of the One justifies the many that are sinners.' In short, long before Luther came on the scene, early Christians read the New Testament as teaching a 'great exchange' in which Christ takes our sin and we receive his righteousness.

This early Christian document does not prove the accuracy of the Reformed reading of Paul. But it does indicate that the Reformed understanding of him did not just arise out of medieval concerns and the Reformers' struggle with Roman Catholicism. The NPP, on the other hand, is without precedent in the history of Christian interpretation and arose at a time when theological liberalism, tolerance and ecumenism were the dominant trends within New Testament scholarship.

Which do we choose — a historic interpretation that has transcended the change of human history, or a modern one that reflects the societal impulses of our age? It is easy to understand how in a post-Holocaust and ecumenical age, the NPP could make such inroads into the evangelical church. We, however, remain exegetically and theologically unconvinced of its accuracy. And we doubt that it will stand the test of time.

NOTES

Introduction

1. Richard Gaffin, 'A Reformed Critique of the New Perspective,' *Modern Reformation,* March/April 2002, p.24.

2. N. T. Wright, *What Saint Paul Really Said: Was Paul of Tarsus the Real Founder of Christianity?* (Grand Rapids, MI: Eerdmans, 1997), p.119.

3. *Ibid.,* p.60.

4. An outstanding example of this is Guy Waters, *Justification and the New Perspectives on Paul* (Phillipsburg, NJ: P and R Publishing, 2004). We strongly recommend Waters' work for those who want to dig deeper. For a plea from within the NPP for recognizing the diversity among its proponents, see N. T. Wright, 'New Perspectives on Paul', delivered at the Tenth Edinburgh Dogmatics Conference, Rutherford House, Edinburgh, August 2003.

5. John Piper, *The Future of Justification: A Response to N. T. Wright* (Wheaton, IL: Crossway Books, 2007). Wright's response to Piper is found in N. T. Wright, *Justification: God's Plan and Paul's Vision* (Downers Grove, IL: InterVarsity Press, 2009).

Chapter 1 — An overview of the New Perspective on Paul

1. Krister Stendahl, 'The Apostle Paul and the Introspective Conscience of the West', reprinted in *Paul among Jews and Gentiles* (Philadelphia: Fortress Press, 1976 [originally published 1963]), pp.78-96. N. T. Wright asserts that this essay 'alerted the world to problems in traditional readings of Paul some while before [E. P.] Sanders' (*What Saint Paul Really Said,* p.190).

2. Stendahl, 'The Apostle Paul and the Introspective Conscience of the West', pp.7-23.

3. E. P. Sanders, *Paul and Palestinian Judaism,* London: SCM Press, 1977.

4. Wright, *What Saint Paul Really Said,* p.20.

5. Cf., e.g., the discussion in J. D. G. Dunn, *The Theology of Paul the Apostle* (Grand Rapids: Eerdmans, 1998), pp.354-9.

6. N. T. Wright is an exception here.

7. Wright, *What Saint Paul Really Said*, p.94.

8. N. T. Wright, 'The Shape of Justification', from the April 2001 Bible Review of the Biblical Archaeological Review website.

9. A phrase originally used by Albert Schweitzer, but repeated in recent discussions. See Schweitzer, *The Mysticism of Paul the Apostle* (New York: Seabury Press, 1931), p.225.

10. Cf. Wright's discussion in *What Saint Paul Really Said*, pp.113-20. For a more detailed discussion, see N. T. Wright, *Justification: God's Plan and Paul's Vision* (Downers Grove, IL: InterVarsity Press, 2009).

11. Wright, *What Saint Paul Really Said*, p.125 (emphasis his).

12. *Ibid.,* pp.158-9; cf. also 'New Perspectives on Paul', p.15.

13. Wright, *What Saint Paul Really Said*, p.98.

14. *Westminster Confession of Faith,* 11.2.

15. It is important to point out Wright's claim that he had already begun to come to many of his conclusions on Paul prior to the publication of Sanders' work, though the latter helped to shape and confirm many of his views. Wright's reading of Paul, as we shall see in chapters 5-6, is actually shaped by his new perspective on the entire Bible, seeing God's goal as reasserting his just rule over creation and God's 'covenant' as primarily having to do with God's creating a single, worldwide family. In this sense, Wright is unique among the NPP, even though he has much in common with Sanders and Dunn.

Chapter 2 — The origin of Paul's Christian life and gospel

1. Wright does not deny the importance of being in a right relationship with God. Yet he sees the Jew/Gentile question as being pre-eminent in Paul's letters. In his opinion, Paul's 'call' must be understood in the light of God's 'covenant' with Abraham, especially that God would make from his seed a worldwide family of believers. We will look at this in greater detail in chapter 5.

2. James D. G. Dunn, 'Paul and Justification by Faith,' in *The Road from Damascus: The Impact of Paul's Conversion on his Life, Thought and Ministry*, ed. R. N. Longenecker (Grand Rapids: Eerdmans, 1997), p.93.

3. *Ibid.,* p.86 (with reference to Stendahl).

4. Cf., e.g., J. D. G. Dunn, *The Theology of Paul the Apostle* (Grand Rapids: Eerdmans, 1998), pp.346-54.

5. Dunn, 'Paul and Justification by Faith', p.94.

6. Some understand Romans 7:14-25 to be a description of Paul's *pre-conversion* struggle with sin, but that interpretation is unlikely. We will return to this passage later.

7. The reference to Paul's kicking 'against the goads' in Acts 26:14 may refer to pre-conversion pangs of conscience.

8. Dunn, 'Paul and Justification by Faith', p.93.

9. Cf., e.g., Wright, *What Saint Paul Really Said,* pp.132, 114-15.

10. *Ibid.,* p.158.

11. *Ibid.,* p.159.

12. *Ibid.,* p.158.

13. Wright, 'New Perspectives on Paul', p.3.

Chapter 3 — Was Paul battling against Jewish legalism?

1. Wright, *What Saint Paul Really Said,* p.20.

2. N. T. Wright, 'The Paul of History and the Apostle of Faith', *Tyndale Bulletin* 29 (1978), pp.61-88.

3. Sanders, *Paul and Palestinian Judaism,* pp.16-18.

4. Cf. *ibid.,* p.125.

5. *Ibid.,* p.147.

6. *Ibid.,* p.xii.

7. *Ibid.,* p.38 (emphasis his).

8. *Ibid.,* p.426.

9. Cf., e.g., Don Garlington, *'The Obedience of Faith': A Pauline Phrase in Historical Context* (Tübingen: J.C.B. Mohr [Paul Siebeck], 1991, who finds the same pattern of covenantal nomism in the Apocrypha.

10. D. A. Carson, Peter O'Brien and Mark Seifrid (eds), *Justification and Variegated Nomism, Volume 1: The Complexities of Second Temple Judaism* (Grand Rapids: Baker, 2001), hereafter referred to as *JVN.*

11. Robert A. Kugler, 'Testaments', *JVN,* pp.189-213.

12. *Ibid.,* pp.196-7.

13. *Ibid.,* p.197.

14. See Craig Evans, 'Scripture-Based Stories in the Pseudepigrapha', *JVN,* pp.57-72.

15. *Ibid.,* p.63.

16. *Ibid.,* p.69.

17. Sanders, *Paul and Palestinian Judaism,* p.423.

18. See, e.g., the didactic stories examined by Philip R. Davies; 'Didactic Stories,' *JVN,* pp.99-133. Cf. especially the *Letter of Aristeas,* where, as D. A. Carson summarizes, 'there is no emphasis [against Sanders] on getting in by God's electing grace…' (*JVN,* p.513).

19. *JVN,* p.98.

20. '1QS and Salvation at Qumran,' *JVN,* p.414.

21. Sanders, *Paul and Palestinian Judaism,* p.422 (emphasis his). According to Sanders, IV Ezra represents 'the closest approach to legalistic works-righteousness which can be found in the Jewish literature of the period' (p.418).

22. Richard Bauckham, 'Apocalypses', *JVN,* p.173.

23. This is consistently attested by the essays in *JVN.*

24. *JVN,* pp.543-4.

25. See Neusner's review in *History of Religions* 18 (1978), pp.177-91.

26. Bauckham, 'Apocalypses', p.174.

27. Carson, 'Summaries and Conclusions', *JVN*, p.545.

28. Stephen Westerholm, *Perspectives Old and New on Paul: The 'Lutheran' Paul and his Critics* (Grand Rapids: Eerdmans, 2004), p.342.

29. Sanders, *Paul and Palestinian Judaism*, p.100.

30. *Ibid.*, p.297.

31. *Ibid.*, p.297. See Westerholm, *Perspectives Old and New on Paul*, p.342.

32. Sanders, *Paul and Palestinian Judaism*, p.87.

33. *Ibid.*, pp.129-30, 139, 141.

34. Peter Enns, 'Expansions of Scripture', *JVN*, p.98.

35. James D. G. Dunn, 'The Justice of God: A Renewed Perspective on Justification by Faith', *Journal of Theological Studies* 43 (1992), pp.7-8.

36. *Ibid.*, p.8.

37. *Trinity Journal*, 25, no. 1 (Spring 2004), pp.111-13.

38. Wright, *What Saint Paul Really Said*, pp.18-19.

39. *Ibid.*, p.19.

40. C. Venema, 'Evaluating the New Perspective on Paul (Question One): Questions Regarding Sanders' View of Second Temple Judaism', *The Outlook*, April 2003, pp.19-20.

41. Sanders, *Paul and Palestinian Judaism*, p.426.

42. This would be true even if the earlier forms of 'boasting' are legitimate, as some scholars believe, just as Paul can refer to legitimate forms of Christian boasting (cf. Rom. 5:2,3,11; the Greek uses the same verbal forms as in chapters 2 – 4, though some English translations do not reflect this).

43. Elsewhere it was said that Abraham kept the whole law before it was given (Qidd. 4:14; Sir. 44:19-21), and that he 'did not sin' against God (Prayer of Manasseh 8).

44. Cf. E. P. Sanders, *Paul, the Law, and the Jewish People* (Philadelphia: Fortress, 1983), pp.32-6; J. D. G. Dunn, *Romans 1-8* (Dallas: Word Books, 1988), pp.185-94.

45. See, for example, Charles Hodge, *A Commentary on Romans* (Carlisle, PA: The Banner of Truth Trust, 1997 [first published 1835]). With regard to 'boasting' in Romans 3:27, Hodge writes, 'The reference ... is not specially to ver. 1 of this chapter, *the* boasting of the Jews over the Gentiles, but *the* boasting of the sinner before God. The latter, however, includes the former. A plan of salvation which strips every man of merit, and places all sinners on the same level before God, of course cuts off all assumption of superiority of one class over another' (p.100).

46. Neither Sanders nor Dunn gives a satisfactory interpretation of these passages. Sanders' denial that Abraham tried to be justified by his works, while correct, misses the point (*Paul, the Law, and the Jewish People*, p.33).

Dunn's interpretation is tied to his understanding of the phrase 'works of the law', which we will deal with in chapter 4.

47. For an alternative reading, cf. T. David Gordon, 'Why Israel Did Not Obtain Torah-Righteousness: A Translation Note on Rom. 9:32', *Westminster Theological Journal* 54 (1992), pp.163-6. Gordon argues that in Romans 9:32 we should not supply the word 'pursue'. Literally, the Greek of verses 31-32 reads, '... but Israel pursuing a law of righteousness did not attain unto law. Why? Because not from faith but as from works.' He argues that the stress of verse 31 and the word order indicate that law is the subject of verse 32 — the law is not from faith, but from works — and translators incorrectly insert 'they pursued it'. This is a possible translation. As we shall see in the next chapter, there is in the law what some have referred to as a 'works-inheritance principle'. But the problem with Gordon's interpretation is the word 'as' in verse 32. It does not make as much sense for Paul to say that the law is 'as from works' as it does to say that Israel's pursuit was not from faith, but as if it were based on works (which is how most translations render it).

48. J. D. G. Dunn, *Romans 9-16* (Dallas: Word, 1988), p.582.

49. *Ibid.,* p.593.

50. *Ibid.,* p.588.

51. Sanders, *Paul, the Law, and the Jewish People,* pp.44-5.

52. *Ibid.,* pp.43-4; cf. pp. 23f.

53. *Ibid.,* p.139-41.

54. According to Sanders, Philippians 3:6,9 indicate that Paul did attain to righteousness, but it was the wrong kind (*ibid.,* p.43).

55. See M. Silva, *Philippians* (Grand Rapids: Baker, 1992), pp.175-6.

Chapter 4 — Covenant, law and 'works of the law' in Paul's theology

1. See the outstanding study of the discussions and debates of the Puritans by Ernest Kevan, *The Grace of Law: A Study in Puritan Theology* (Grand Rapids: Baker, 1976).

2. See, e.g., N. T. Wright, *The Climax of the Covenant: Christ and the Law in Pauline Theology* (Minneapolis: Fortress Press, 1991), pp.193-216.

3. See the discussions of Cranfield, *Romans,* vol. 1, p.364, and Murray, *Romans,* vol. 1, pp.264-8.

4. O. Palmer Robertson, *The Christ of the Covenants* (Grand Rapids: Baker, 1980), p.4.

5. James Buchanan, *The Doctrine of Justification: An Outline of its History in the Church and of its Exposition from Scripture* (Carlisle, PA: The Banner of Truth Trust, 1961 [first published 1867]), p.39.

6. On this point, see Kevan, *The Grace of Law,* pp.118-19.

7. This last statement demands comment, especially in the light of the many modern translations that read Galatians 3:24 in the temporal sense

that the law was our guardian 'until Christ came' (ESV; RSV; NRSV; NLT). The key issue is how to translate the Greek preposition *eis*, which typically describes motion towards or into something. But it can also take on other meanings. It has the temporal meaning of 'until' in verse 23. But in that instance we have a clear temporal marker within the prepositional phrase. The temporal use of *eis* is infrequent, and, as Burton points out, when it is used in that sense it usually takes a temporal object (Ernest Burton, *Galatians,* ICC; T&T Clark, 1975), p.200. That is not the case in verse 24. Thus we prefer the traditional reading — the law leads us to Christ.

8. John Calvin, *Epistle of Paul the Apostle to the Romans* (Calvin's Commentaries, vol. 19; Grand Rapids: Baker, 1979), p.383f.

9. R. L. Dabney, *Systematic Theology* (Edinburgh: The Banner of Truth Trust, 2002 [first published 1878]) p.457.

10. See the paper by Steve Baugh, 'Galatians 5:1-6 and Personal Obligation: Reflections on Paul and the Law', delivered at the annual meeting of the Evangelical Theological Society, San Antonio, TX, November 2004.

11. From the hymn 'Thy works, not mine, O Christ', by Horatius Bonar, 1857.

12. See John Stott, *The Message of Galatians* (Downers Grove, IL: IVP, 1968), p.92.

13. James Dunn, *The Epistle to the Galatians* (Peabody, MA: Hendrickson, 1993), p.190.

14. Murray, *Romans,* vol. 1, p.208.

15. E.g., C. E. B. Cranfield, *A Critical and Exegetical Commentary on the Epistle to the Romans* (Edinburgh: T and T Clark, 1975), vol. 1, pp.292-3.

16. E.g., John Murray, *The Epistle to the Romans* (Grand Rapids: Eerdmans, 1959), vol. 1, pp.207-8.

17. On this interpretation, see D. Moo, *The Epistle to the Romans* (Grand Rapids: Eerdmans, 1996), pp.347-9.

18. See the excellent article by C. E. B. Cranfield, 'Has the Old Testament Law a Place in the Christian Life? A Response to Professor Westerholm,' *Irish Biblical Studies* 15 (1993), pp.50-64.

19. Gal. 2:16 (three times); 3:2,5,10; Rom. 3:20,28.

20. Dunn, *Romans 1-8,* p.158.

21. Dunn, 'The New Perspective on Paul,' *BJRL* 65 (1983), p.110.

22. Cf. Dunn, *The Theology of Paul the Apostle,* p.358; *Galatians,* p.136. For this reading, see also Wright, *The Climax of the Covenant,* pp.144-8 (works demanded by the law). This aspect of Dunn's interpretation is sometimes missed by his critics. Cf., e.g., Dunn's response to Cranfield, 'Yet Once More — "The Works of the Law": A Response,' in *JSNT* 46 (1992), pp.99-117.

23. Dunn, *The Theology of Paul the Apostle,* pp.361-2; *Galatians,* p.172.

24. Dunn, *The Theology of Paul the Apostle*, p.361.
25. *Ibid.*, p.13, n.39.

Chapter 5 — Justification by Faith and N. T. Wright's narrative reading of the Bible

1. Wright, *What Saint Paul Really Said*, p.20.
2. N. T. Wright, *The New Testament and the People of God* (Minneapolis: Fortress Press, 1992), p.202. Throughout this work, Wright regularly refers to 'god', with a lower case 'g', not a capital 'G'. He gives his reasons for this on pages xiv-xv.
3. *Ibid.*, p.99.
4. *Ibid.*, p.336.
5. *Ibid.*, pp.336-7.
6. *Ibid.*, p.405.
7. *Ibid.*, p.246.
8. Wright, *What Saint Paul Really Said*, p.132.
9. *Ibid.*, p.60.
10. N. T. Wright, *Paul: In Fresh Perspective* (Minneapolis: Fortress Press, 2005), p.10.
11. *Ibid.*, p.12 (emphasis his).
12. Wright, *What Saint Paul Really Said*, p.119.
13. *Ibid.*, p.94.
14. Wright, 'The Shape of Justification'.
15. Wright, *What Saint Paul Really Said*, p.113.
16. *Ibid.*, pp.158-9.
17. N. T. Wright, *The Letter to the Romans*, The New Interpreter's Bible, vol. X (Nashville: Abingdon Press, 2002) p.485.
18. Wright, *The New Testament and the People of God*, p.38.
19. *Ibid.*, p.36.
20. *Ibid.*, p.65 (emphasis his).
21. *Ibid.*, p.38.
22. Wright, *Paul: In Fresh Perspective*, p.20.
23. *Ibid.*, p.21.
24. *Ibid.*, p.24.
25. Wright, *The New Testament and the People of God*, p.43.
26. *Ibid.*, pp.369-70.
27. Cf., e.g., *Paul: In Fresh Perspective*, p.12.
28. Wright, *The New Testament and the People of God*, p.258.
29. Cf. e.g., Wright, *Paul: In Fresh Perspective*, pp.7-8.
30. Wright, *Justification*, p.65.
31. *Ibid.*, p.67.
32. *Ibid.*
33. Wright, *The Climax of the Covenant*, p.214.

34. See the helpful, yet overly positive, review of *The Climax of the Covenant* by T. David Gordon, *Westminster Theological Journal*, 56 no. 1, Spring 1994, pp. 197-201.

35. Wright, *The Climax of the Covenant*, p.23.

36. *Ibid.*, p.61 (emphasis his).

Chapter 6 — Justification by faith: the biblical doctrine

1. Wright, 'The Shape of Justification'. See also chapter 7 of *What Saint Paul Really Said*.

2. Piper, *The Future of Justification*, p.86.

3. Most commentators agree that Paul's opponents were professing Christians, who taught that Paul left out some parts of 'the gospel' when he preached in Galatia. Those who did not believe in Jesus as Lord would not have made the inroads that the false teachers did.

4. Wright, *What Saint Paul Really Said*, p.158.

5. *Ibid.*, p.159.

6. Wright, 'New Perspectives on Paul', p.3.

7. Charles E. Hill, *Third Millennium Magazine Online* 3:22 (28 May – 2 June 2001). Available at:
http://www.thirdmill.org/files/english/html/nt/NT.h.Hill.Wright.html.

8. See the discussion of Brian Vickers, *Jesus' Blood and Righteousness*, Crossway, 2006, pp.83-4.

9. Mark Seifrid, 'Righteousness Language in the Hebrew Scriptures and Early Judaism', *JVN*, vol. 1, p.423.

10. *Ibid.*, p.424.

11. *Ibid.*

12. Wright, *Romans*, p.491.

13. Vickers, *Jesus' Blood and Righteousness*, p.85.

14. As Vickers points out (*Jesus' Blood and Righteousness*, p 83), this fits with biblical examples of one thing being reckoned as something else, as when Laban 'reckons' his daughters as foreigners (Gen. 31:15).

15. Vickers, *Jesus' Blood and Righteousness*, pp.85-6.

16. Wright, *Romans*, p.424 (emphasis his).

17. *Wright, Justification.* p.9.

18. Some, especially in the Lutheran tradition, have held to the imputation of Christ's 'passive obedience' — that is, his obedience in his death on the cross. But the predominant position in the 'Reformed' tradition has been the imputation of the active obedience of Christ.

19. Ecclesiastes 7:29 states, 'God made man upright, but they have sought out many schemes.' The Hebrew word translated 'upright' (*yashar*) is not the normal word translated 'righteous' (*tsaddiq*), but the use of 'righteous' in the surrounding context (Eccles. 7:15,16,20; 8:14; 9:1-2) indicates that they are synonyms. In fact, in this context 'righteous' clearly refers to

meeting a moral standard, as it is consistently contrasted with the 'wicked' and with sin; cf. Ecclesiastes 7:20: 'Surely there is not a righteous man on earth who does good and never sins.'

20. Wright, *Justification,* p.95.

21. Wright, *What Saint Paul Really Said,* p.102.

22. See note 8 above for details.

23. Vickers, *Jesus' Blood and Righteousness,* pp.85-6.

24. *Ibid.,* p.86.

25. In Romans 5:13, Paul uses the language of 'reckoning' or 'imputing': 'for until the Law sin was in the world, but sin is not imputed when there is no law' (NASB). In other words, Paul is saying that, until the law comes, 'sin' is not charged to people's account. It is only when the law comes, and sin becomes 'transgression', this it is legally charged. He made a similar point in Romans 4:15: 'For the law brings wrath, but where there is no law there is no transgression.'

Yet, Paul goes on to say in 5:14, this does not mean that all who lived before the law was given go through life blissfully innocent. They die and face condemnation: 'Yet death reigned from Adam to Moses, even over those whose sinning was not like the transgression of Adam, who was a type of the one who was to come.' But if their sin was not reckoned to their account, how can they be condemned?

There is only one answer: Adam's sin was imputed to them. Death / condemnation is because of Adam's sin imputed to all.

26. Wright, *What Saint Paul Really Said,* pp.104-5. Cf. Wright, 'On Becoming the Righteousness of God: 2 Corinthians 5:2.', in *Pauline Theology, Volume 2: 1 and 2 Corinthians,* ed. D. M. Hay (Minneapolis: Fortress), pp.200-208.

27. Vickers, *Jesus' Blood and Righteousness,* p.182 (emphasis his).

28. Wright, *What Saint Paul Really Said,* pp.98-9 (emphasis his).

29. Piper, *The Future of Justification,* p.79.

30. Wright, *Justification,* pp.231-2.

31. *Ibid.* (emphasis his).

32. Buchanan, *The Doctrine of Justification,* p.39.

33. Wright, *Justification,* pp.232-3.

34. *Ibid.,* p.233.

35. Wright, 'Paul in Different Perspectives: Lecture 1: Starting Points and Opening Reflections', at the Pastors' Conference of Auburn Avenue Presbyterian Church, Monroe, Louisiana (3 January 2005).

36. See William B. Barcley, *'Christ in You': A Study in Paul's Theology and Ethics* (Lanham, MD: University Press of America, 1999).

37. Wright, *What Saint Paul Really Said,* p.160.

38. Piper, *The Future of Justification,* p.131 (emphasis his).

39. Wright, 'New Perspectives on Paul', p.253.

40. Wright, *Paul: In Fresh Perspective*, p.121.
41. Wright, *What Saint Paul Really Said*, p.129.
42. Wright, 'New Perspectives on Paul', p.260.
43. *Ibid.,* p.254.
44. Wright, *Paul in Fresh Perspective*, p.148.
45. Wright, *Justification,* p.237.
46. *Ibid.,* p.239.
47. *Ibid.*
48. Wright, 'New Perspectives on Paul', p.254.
49. Wright, *What Saint Paul Really Said,* p.113.

INDEX

Qumran community, the, 55, 96

reckoning — see 'imputation'
Reformers, the (the Reformation; see also 'Luther, Martin'), 9, 50, 61
theology of, 14, 15, 23, 24, 27,
28, 37, 57, 60, 61-2, 74, 80,
82, 83, 87, 90, 94, 109, 118,
119, 121, 125, 132-5, 138,
148, 156, 159, 161, 163,
164, 165, 166, 182
traditional interpretation of
Paul, 9, 11, 21, 22, 25, 28,
30, 50, 67, 95, 97, 100, 112,
119, 129, 130, 132, 148,
170, 171, 173
regeneration, 164
righteousness (see also 'justification'), 11, 31, 38-9, 67-71,
98, 99, 126, 141-60, 182-3
a gift, 146, 147, 153, 154
by works — see 'works-
righteousness'
God clothes his people with,
150
imparted, 158
imputation of Christ's, 27,
89-90, 102, 128, 132, 133,
134, 148-60, 166
Wright's criticisms of (see
also 'Wright, denial of
imputation of Christ's
righteousness'), 152-60
Israel's pursuit of, 67-8, 87,
179
moral dimension of, 142,
143-4, 147-8
occurrences of the term, 142
of God, 9-10, 26, 44, 67, 68-9,
108, 135, 136, 139, 143,
145-7, 154, 166

reckoned to Abraham, 143-4,
147-8, 149, 153
standard that God demands,
85, 98, 99, 149, 150, 155
under the law, 18, 35, 36 69,
70, 71, 147
Wright's definition of, 44,
132, 139, 141-8, 171
Roman Catholicism, 9, 10, 17,
27, 28, 50, 61, 112, 151, 170,
173

sacrifices, 11, 20, 23, 37, 43, 52,
84, 87, 99, 101, 115, 126, 157
salvation, 10, 12, 13, 15, 21, 22,
23, 24, 26, 40-42, 46, 47, 55,
56, 57, 58, 59, 60, 61, 64, 70,
71, 73, 74, 84, 88, 98, 99, 104,
109, 112, 118, 120, 125, 131,
136, 137, 150, 152, 164, 168,
170
Wright's view of, 106, 107,
109-10, 118, 119, 131, 152
sanctification, 79, 164
Sanders, E. P., 12, 19-21, 23, 24,
25, 27, 35, 50-63, 66, 70, 87,
95, 104, 110, 175, 176, 178,
179
Seifrid, Mark, 142
semi-Pelagianism, 61, 160, 164
sin, 44-5, 64, 90-94, 95, 117,
118-19, 152, 158, 171-3, 183
effects of, 36, 40-41, 117, 118,
119, 127, 128, 129, 134, 135
God's wrath against, 36, 41,
43, 45, 66, 100, 131, 134,
136, 140, 167, 170
problem of, 9-10, 18, 19, 23,
24, 25, 28, 34, 35-7, 40-42,
44, 45, 47, 49, 93, 98, 105,
114, 117, 121, 128, 134,
167-8

We are indebted to Barcley and Duncan for providing a clear, understandable and accessible explanation and critique of the NPP.

Robert J. Cara, Ph.D.,
Chief Academic Officer, Hugh and Sallie Reaves Professor of New Testament, RTS Charlotte

Barcley and Duncan remind us that the fundamental need of sinners is to be reconciled with God, and that our only hope for such a right standing with God is the righteousness of Jesus Christ. The New Perspective on Paul misunderstands the meaning of justification and fails to see its centrality. Barcley and Duncan in this lucid work provide a clear exposition of the gospel and a needed corrective to the New Perspective on Paul.

Thomas R. Schreiner,
James Buchanan Harrison Professor of New Testament Interpretation, The Southern Baptist Theological Seminary

Bill Barcley and Ligon Duncan combine biblical scholarship and pastoral skill in addressing one of the crucial issues of our time — the doctrine of justification. With enviable clarity and precision, this book adds to the growing number of titles addressing the 'New Perspective(s) on Paul'. At stake is the understanding of the gospel itself. This is the finest summary available of the core issues and a welcome confirmation of the 'old' perspective.

Gospel-driven churches should make this book a special study.

Derek W. H. Thomas,
John E. Richards Professor of Systematic and Practical Theology, RTS Jackson

Justification is perhaps the hallmark doctrine of Protestantism and has thus been over the years the focus of much debate. In recent years a number of scholars have offered sophisticated critiques of the Protestant position, critiques that have become known as 'the New Perspective on Paul'. For the ordinary Christian, many of the arguments seem obscure and of limited relevance; for that reason, it is a pleasure to recommend this book by two pastor-scholars who not only understand the arguments, but also the immediate significance of these issues for the person in the pew. Highly recommended.

Carl Trueman,
Professor of Historical Theology and Church History,
Westminster Seminary, Philadelphia

In recent years, the 'New Perspective on Paul' has become a hot topic of conversation within the evangelical church. What is the new perspective? Is it an important issue for the church's reflection? What should evangelicals think about it? We may be grateful to Drs Barcley and Duncan for providing a sure guide to navigating the often challenging waters of the new perspective. This fine book provides the reader new to these discussions with a fair-minded overview and engagement of the new perspective. Readers already familiar with the new perspective will find much biblical and theological food for thought in this volume. If you are looking for a recent and Reformed response to the new perspective, this is the book for you.

Guy Waters,
Associate Professor of New Testament, RTS Jackson